Simply Anti-Inflammatory: 96 Easy 5-Ingredient Recipes

Gourmet Heritage Passage

Contents

INTRODUCTION

Welcome to the world of delicious anti-inflammatory recipes! In Simply Anti-Inflammatory: 96 Easy 5-Ingredient Recipes, we strive to provide you with the most delicious, easy to make, and healthfully nutritious recipes that won't leave your wallet feeling empty.

This cookbook provides a range of mouth-watering recipes that include only five ingredients or less. Whether you are looking for a quick and easy starter, main course or dessert, this book has something for every inclined cook. The added bonus is that each recipe also helps fighting inflammation and improving your overall wellbeing.

The recipes are as varied as they are easy to make. Our main course dishes feature flavorful blends of proteins, vegetables, herbs and spices. Our deliciously nutritious breakfast and snack recipes will help you start your day off right and tide you over until the next meal. For dinner time, you'll find a host of easy to prepare recipes including soups, stews, chili, casseroles and stir-fries. Finally, our dessert recipes are sure to satisfy your sweet tooth while not sacrificing nutrition.

This book also includes a section on understanding the benefits of anti-inflammatory foods and how to incorporate them into your cooking. In addition, we provide nutritional information for each dish, so you can make informed choices. We also supply allergy-specific ingredient substitutions.

With this cookbook, you'll be able to swiftly put together delicious anti-inflammatory meals with ease. So what are you waiting for? Let's get cooking and enjoy the health-promoting goodness that anti-inflammatory foods provide. Bon appetit!

1. Turmeric Ginger Tea

Turmeric Ginger Tea is a flavorful and comforting blend of herbs and spices with natural anti-inflammatory benefits and a delicious aroma. This beverage is perfect for chilly mornings or cozy evenings.
Serving: 3 cups
Preparation Time: 10 minutes
Ready time: 10 minutes

Ingredients:
- 4 cups water
- 2 teaspoons freshly grated ginger
- 1 teaspoon freshly grated turmeric
- 1 teaspoon honey
- A pinch of black pepper

Instructions:
1. Bring the water to a boil in a medium-sized pot over medium-high heat.
2. Add the ginger, turmeric and black pepper to the boiling water and lower the heat to a simmer.
3. Let the tea simmer for 10 minutes.
4. Strain the tea into mugs and add the honey. Stir to combine.

Nutrition information:
Calories: 28
Protein: 0.6g
Sugar: 2.8g
Fat: 0.1g
Carbohydrates: 6.1g

2. Baked Salmon with Lemon and Dill

Baked Salmon with Lemon and Dill is a flavorful and simple to make seafood dinner that is perfect for weeknight meals or entertaining. It uses just a handful of Ingredients and infuses the salmon with the flavors of fresh lemon, garlic, and herbs.

Serving: Serves 2-4
Preparation time: 10 minutes
Ready time: 25 minutes

Ingredients:
4 salmon fillets
2 cloves garlic, crushed
1/4 cup fresh dill, chopped
1 lemon, sliced
2 tablespoons butter
Salt and pepper to taste

Instructions:
1. Preheat oven to 400 degrees F. Grease a 9x13 inch baking dish with butter or cooking spray.
2. Place salmon fillets in the prepared dish.
3. Sprinkle the garlic, dill, and lemon slices over the top of the fillets.
4. Spread the butter over the top of the fillets and season with salt and pepper.
5. Bake in preheated oven for 20-25 minutes, or until the salmon is cooked through and easily flakes with a fork.

Nutrition information:
Calories: 426; Fat: 27g; Saturated fat: 11g; Cholesterol: 111mg; Sodium: 145mg; Carbohydrates: 4g; Protein: 44g.

3. Quinoa Salad with Avocado and Tomato

This vibrant and healthy Quinoa Salad with Avocado and Tomato is perfect as a light lunch or side salad. Filled with fresh tomato, creamy avocado, garlic and a simple tangy dressing, it's a delicious way to introduce more quinoa and vegetables into your diet.
Serving: 4
Preparation time: 10 minutes
Ready time: 10 minutes

Ingredients:
•1 cup of quinoa

- 1 large tomato, diced
- 1 large avocado, diced
- 1 small red onion, diced
- 2 cloves of garlic, minced
- 2 tbsp olive oil
- 2 tbsp red wine vinegar
- 1/2 tsp salt
- Ground black pepper to taste

Instructions:
1. Prepare the quinoa according to the directions on the package.
2. In a large bowl, combine the cooked quinoa, tomato, avocado, red onion, and garlic.
3. In a small bowl, whisk together the olive oil, red wine vinegar, salt, and black pepper.
4. Pour the dressing over the quinoa mixture and toss to combine.
5. Serve the quinoa salad cold or at room temperature.

Nutrition information:
Calories: 286 kcal, Carbohydrates: 21.7 g, Protein: 5.4 g, Fat: 20.3 g, Saturated Fat: 2.9 g, Sodium: 315 mg, Potassium: 455 mg, Fiber: 6.1 g, Sugar: 2.3 g, Vitamin A: 505 IU, Vitamin C: 15.5 mg, Calcium: 24 mg, Iron: 1.8 mg

4. Roasted Turmeric Cauliflower

Roasted Turmeric Cauliflower is an easy side dish that is bursting with flavor and nutrition. The roasted vegetables, lightly coated in an aromatic turmeric spice blend, are a delicious and healthy way to boost your daily intake of vegetables.
Serving: 6
Preparation Time: 10 minutes
Ready Time: 35 minutes

Ingredients:
- 2 heads of cauliflower, cut into florets
- 1/4 cup extra-virgin olive oil
- 1 tablespoon ground turmeric

- 1 teaspoon garlic powder
- 1/2 teaspoon paprika
- Salt and pepper, to taste

Instructions:
1. Preheat oven to 425°F/ 220°C.
2. On a baking sheet, toss the cauliflower florets with olive oil, turmeric, garlic powder, paprika, and salt and pepper.
3. Roast in preheated oven until golden brown, about 25-30 minutes.
4. Serve hot with or without additional seasoning, if desired.

Nutrition information:Serving (1/6 of a head of cauliflower), Calories: 93, Carbohydrates: 9g, Fat: 7g, Fiber: 4g, Protein: 3g

5. Blueberry Chia Seed Pudding

Blueberry Chia Seed Pudding is a refreshing and nutritiously balanced breakfast or snack. Filled with healthy antioxidants from the blues combined with the protein and fiber-rich chia seeds, this pudding will fill you up and make you feel energized.
Serving: 2
Preparation Time: 10 mins
Ready Time: 4 hrs

Ingredients:
-2 tablespoons of chia seeds
-3/4 cup of fresh blueberries
-1/2 cup of plant-based milk
-1 teaspoon of pure maple syrup
-2 teaspoons of vanilla extract

Instructions:
1. Combine chia seeds with 1/2 cup of plant-based milk, maple syrup, and vanilla extract in a medium-sized bowl.
2. The mixture should become thick, if it's too thin, add more chia seeds and stir.
3. Rinse the blueberries and add them to the mixture.
4. Mix everything together and pour the mixture into two jars.

5. Place the jars in the refrigerator and let them set for 4 hours.
6. Serve the pudding cold with additional fresh blueberries, nut butter, and nuts.

Nutrition information (per serving):
Calories: 90 kcal, Carbohydrates: 11 g, Protein: 2 g, Fat: 5 g, Saturated Fat: 0 g, Cholesterol: 0 mg, Sodium: 21 mg, Potassium: 72 mg, Fiber: 3 g, Sugar: 7 g, Vitamin A: 1.3%, Vitamin C: 16.3%, Calcium: 4.3%, Iron: 2.6%

6. Spinach and Mushroom Omelette

Spinach and Mushrooms Omelette is a simple, delicious, and nutritious breakfast that can be cooked in just a few minutes. It is a great way to enjoy the health benefits of spinach and mushrooms while also adding some protein to your meal.
Serving: 2 servings
Preparation time: 10 minutes
Ready time: 10 minutes

Ingredients:
- 2 eggs
- 2 cups baby spinach, chopped
- 1/2 cup white mushrooms, sliced
- 2 tablespoons olive oil
- Salt and pepper, to taste

Instructions:
1. Heat the olive oil in a large skillet over medium heat.
2. Add the mushrooms and cook until softened, about 2 minutes.
3. Add the spinach and cook until softened, about 2 more minutes.
4. In a medium bowl, whisk together the eggs, salt and pepper.
5. Add the egg mixture to the skillet and reduce the heat to low.
6. Cook the omelette, covered, until the bottom is lightly golden, about 4 minutes.
7. Flip the omelette and cook, covered, until set, about 4 more minutes.
8. Remove from the heat and enjoy!

Nutrition information:
Calories: 250, Fat: 18g, Carbohydrates: 3g, Protein:17g, Fiber: 2g, Sugar: 1g.

7. Grilled Chicken with Herbs

This delicious Grilled Chicken with Herbs is a classic favorite for lunch or dinner. It's packed with flavor thanks to a blend of aromatic herbs and a handy seasoning mix. Served with vegetables or a simple salad, it makes for a tasty dish that everyone will love.
Serving: 4 servings
Preparation Time: 10 minutes
Ready Time: 20 minutes

Ingredients:
4 chicken breasts
2 tablespoons olive oil
1/2 teaspoon garlic powder
1 teaspoon garlic granules
1 teaspoon paprika
1 teaspoon oregano
1/2 teaspoon rosemary
Salt and pepper to taste

Instructions:
1. Preheat the grill to medium heat.
2. In a medium bowl, combine the olive oil, garlic powder, garlic granules, paprika, oregano, rosemary, and salt and pepper.
3. Coat the chicken breasts thoroughly in the mixture.
4. Place the chicken breasts on the preheated grill. Grill for approximately 10 minutes on each side or until the chicken is cooked through.
5. Remove the chicken from the grill and serve with vegetables and/or a simple salad. Enjoy!

Nutrition information: Per serving: calories 266, fat 10 g, cholesterol 97 mg, sodium 114 mg, carbohydrate 2 g, protein 37 g.

8. Cucumber and Tomato Salad

A refreshing cucumber & tomato salad with a zesty dressing is a delicious accompaniment to just about any meal.
Serving: Serves 4
Preparation time: 10 minutes
Ready time: 10 minutes

Ingredients:
• 3 tomatoes, chopped
• 2 cucumbers, sliced
• 1/4 cup red onion, diced
• 1/4 cup fresh parsley leaves, chopped
• 2 tablespoons olive oil
• 2 tablespoons white wine vinegar
• 1/2 teaspoon salt
• 1/4 teaspoon black pepper

Instructions:
1. In a large bowl, combine the tomatoes, cucumbers, red onion, and parsley.
2. In a small bowl, whisk together the olive oil, vinegar, salt, and black pepper.
3. Pour the dressing over the salad and toss to combine.
4. Serve immediately or store in the refrigerator.

Nutrition information: Calories: 127, Fat: 9g, Protein: 1.5g, Carbs: 10.5g, Fiber: 2.4g, Sugar: 5.7g, Sodium: 306mg

9. Baked Sweet Potato Fries

Baked Sweet Potato Fries is a tasty treat that makes for a great snack or side dish. Its crunchy deliciousness and sweet flavor make it an irresistible dish for everyone.
Serving: 4
Preparation Time: 10 minutes
Ready Time: 30 minutes

Ingredients:
- 2 medium sweet potatoes, peeled and cut into thin fries
- 2 tablespoons olive oil
- 2 teaspoons garlic powder
- ¼ teaspoon salt
- ¼ teaspoon black pepper

Instructions:
1. Preheat oven to 375°F (190°C).
2. Place the sweet potato fries on a baking sheet.
3. Drizzle with olive oil and sprinkle with garlic powder, salt, and pepper.
4. Toss to coat evenly.
5. Bake in preheated oven for 25–30 minutes, turning once halfway through, or until crispy and golden.

Nutrition information: Per serving: Calories 152, Total Fat 7 g (Saturated 0 g, Trans 0 g), Cholesterol 0 mg, Sodium 279 mg, Total Carbohydrate 20 g (Dietary Fiber 3 g, Sugars 5 g), Protein 2 g.

10. Ginger Garlic Stir-Fry with Tofu

This delicious stir-fry combines firm, spiced tofu with crunchy vegetables and a flavorful ginger garlic sauce. Perfect for a quick and easy vegan dinner, this dish is sure to become a family favorite.
Serving: Serves 4
Preparation time: 20 minutes
Ready time: 25 minutes

Ingredients:
- 2 tablespoons neutral oil
- 2 (14-ounce) packages super-firm tofu, drained and pressed
- 2 tablespoons Sriracha
- 2 tablespoons low-sodium tamari or soy sauce
- 2 cloves garlic, minced
- 1 tablespoon grated fresh ginger
- 2 cups broccoli florets
- 1 red bell pepper, sliced

- 1/3 cup vegetable broth
- 1 tablespoon cornstarch
- 2 tablespoons toasted sesame oil
- Salt, to taste
- Cooked rice, to serve

Instructions:
1. Heat the oil in a large, deep skillet over medium-high heat.
2. Slice the tofu into cubes and add to the skillet. Cook until golden brown and slightly crisp, about 5 minutes.
3. Meanwhile, mix together the Sriracha, tamari, garlic, and ginger in a small bowl.
4. Add the broccoli and bell pepper to the skillet with the tofu. Pour in the Sriracha mixture and stir everything to combine. Cook for an additional 3 minutes, or until the vegetables are slightly softened.
5. In a separate bowl, whisk together the vegetable broth and cornstarch.
6. Pour the mixture into the skillet and stir everything to combine. Cook for an additional 2 minutes, or until the sauce has thickened.
7. Add the sesame oil and season with salt, to taste.
8. Serve the stir-fry over cooked rice, if desired.

Nutrition information
540 calories, 25.9g fat, 47.8g carbs, 19.8g protein

11. Kale and Berry Smoothie

This Kale and Berry Smoothie is a nutritious and delicious way to get your daily nutrients and a burst of natural energy! Featuring fresh kale and an assortment of sweet berries, it's an ideal way to start your day or replenish after a workout.
Serving: Makes 1 Serving: Preparation Time: 5 minutes
Ready Time: 5 minutes

Ingredients:
• ½ cup fresh kale
• ¾ cup mixed frozen berries
• 1 banana
• ½ cup almond milk

Instructions:

1. Place kale, frozen berries, banana, and almond milk in a blender.
2. Blend until smooth.
3. Serve immediately.

Nutrition information: Per serving, this smoothie contains 230 calories, 7.5g fat, 48g carbohydrates, 7g fiber, and 5g protein.

12. Roasted Brussels Sprouts with Balsamic Glaze

Roasted Brussels Sprouts with Balsamic Glaze is a simple yet flavorful side dish that is sure to impress your guests.
Serving: 4 servings
Preparation Time: 10 minutes
Ready Time: 25 minutes

Ingredients:

- 3 cups Brussels sprouts, halved
- 1/4 cup olive oil
- 2 cloves garlic, minced
- 2 tablespoons balsamic vinegar
- 1 teaspoon honey
- Salt and pepper, to taste

Instructions:

1. Preheat oven to 400°F (205°C).
2. Place Brussels sprouts, olive oil, garlic, balsamic vinegar, honey, salt and pepper on a large baking tray and carefully toss to combine.
3. Roast in the preheated oven for 20-25 minutes, stirring every 10 minutes, until the Brussels sprouts are golden and tender.
4. Serve hot.

Nutrition information:

Calories: 141kcal; Carbohydrates: 8g; Protein: 3g; Fat: 11g; Saturated Fat: 1.5g; Sodium: 37mg; Potassium: 258mg; Fiber: 3g; Sugar: 3g; Vitamin A: 545IU; Vitamin C: 60.5mg; Calcium: 22mg; Iron: 1.4mg.

13. Lemon Garlic Shrimp Skewers

This delicious yet easy-to-make recipe is perfect for any time of year. The combination of the tangy lemon and garlic flavors perfectly complemented by the savory taste of shrimp make Lemon Garlic Shrimp Skewers an excellent dish to prepare for any occasion!

Serving: 4
Preparation time: 10 minutes
Ready time: 25 minutes

Ingredients:
• 2 tablespoons olive oil
• 2 cloves garlic, minced
• 1 tablespoon freshly squeezed lemon juice
• 1/2 teaspoon sea salt
• 1/4 teaspoon freshly ground black pepper
• 2 pounds medium shrimp, peeled and deveined
• 12 to 16 bamboo skewers

Instructions:
1. Preheat the oven to 400°F (200°C).
2. In a medium bowl, combine the olive oil, garlic, lemon juice, salt, and pepper. Add the shrimp and toss to coat.
3. Thread the shrimp onto the bamboo skewers. Place the skewers on a large baking sheet and bake for 10 to 12 minutes, or until the shrimp are cooked through.
4. Remove from the oven and serve.

Nutrition information (per serving): Calories: 187, Total fat: 6g, Saturated fat: 1g, Cholesterol: 217mg, Sodium: 368mg, Carbohydrates: 2g, Fiber: 0g, Sugars: 0g, Protein: 28g

14. Avocado and Tomato Salad

Avocado and Tomato Salad is a fresh and light summer salad, perfect for any meal. It features refreshing avocado, sweet tomatoes, and a light citrus-based dressing.

Serving: 4 people
Preparation Time: 15 minutes
Ready Time: 15 minutes

Ingredients:
- 2 large avocados, diced
- 2 large tomatoes, diced
- Juice of 1 lime
- 2 tablespoons olive oil
- 2 cloves garlic, minced
- 1/4 teaspoon ground cumin
- Salt, to taste

Instructions:
1. In a medium-sized bowl, combine the diced avocados and tomatoes.
2. In a separate small bowl, whisk together the lime juice, olive oil, garlic, cumin, and salt.
3. Pour the dressing over the avocado and tomato mixture and stir until everything is evenly coated.
4. Refrigerate for at least 15 minutes before serving.

Nutrition information:
Calories: 232, Fat: 18.9g, Saturated fat: 2.6g, Cholesterol: 0mg, Sodium: 7mg, Potassium: 816mg, Carbohydrates: 14.4g, Fiber: 6.7g, Sugar: 3.8g, Protein: 2.6g

15. Turmeric Roasted Chickpeas

Turmeric Roasted Chickpeas are a delicious and healthy snack or side dish, with an earthy, nutty flavor and a pleasant crunch. Serve with a green salad or as part of a larger Middle Eastern-style spread.
Serving: 6
Preparation Time: 10 minutes
Ready Time: 40 minutes

Ingredients:
-1 can chickpeas, drained and rinsed
-1 tablespoon olive oil

-1 teaspoon ground cumin
-1 teaspoon ground turmeric
-1/2 teaspoon ground coriander
-1/2 teaspoon garlic powder
-1/2 teaspoon paprika
-Salt and freshly ground black pepper, to taste

Instructions:
1. Preheat the oven to 400°F (200°C).
2. Line a baking sheet with parchment paper.
3. In a bowl, combine the chickpeas, olive oil, cumin, turmeric, coriander, garlic powder, paprika, and salt and pepper. Stir until the chickpeas are evenly coated.
4. Spread the chickpeas in a single layer onto the baking sheet.
5. Bake for 20 minutes, then stir the chickpeas and bake for an additional 20 minutes, or until golden brown and crispy.
6. Let cool before serving.

Nutrition information: Calories: 79, Total Fat: 3g, Saturated Fat: 0g, Trans Fat: 0g, Cholesterol: 0mg, Sodium: 107mg, Carbohydrates: 11g, Dietary Fiber: 3g, Sugars: 1g, Protein: 3g

16. Broccoli and Quinoa Stir-Fry

This delicious and nutritious Broccoli and Quinoa Stir-Fry is easy to make and perfect for a weeknight dinner. Served with any type of protein, it's sure to be a family favorite.
Serving: 4
Preparation time: 10 minutes
Ready time: 20 minutes

Ingredients:
• 2 cups diced broccoli
• ½ cup dry quinoa
• 1 teaspoon minced garlic
• 1 teaspoon sesame oil
• 2 tablespoons soy sauce or coconut aminos
• 1 teaspoon fresh ginger, minced

• 2 tablespoons olive oil

Instructions:
1. Begin by cooking the quinoa according to package Instructions.
2. Heat the olive oil over medium-high heat in a large skillet.
3. Add the garlic and ginger to the skillet and sauté for a minute or two, stirring frequently.
4. Add the diced broccoli and sauté until the broccoli is tender, about 5-7 minutes.
5. Add the cooked quinoa, sesame oil and soy sauce/coconut aminos and stir to combine. Cook an additional 2-3 minutes.
6. Serve hot, with a protein of choice if desired.

Nutrition information:
• Calories: 189 kcal
• Carbohydrates: 19.7g
• Protein: 6.7g
• Fat: 9.2g
• Saturated Fat: 1.4g
• Sodium: 400mg
• Fiber: 3.4g
• Sugar: 1.6g

17. Mixed Berry Parfait with Greek Yogurt

This Mixed Berry Parfait with Greek Yogurt is a simple, protein-packed dessert that can be made in no time. It is a light and refreshing way to satisfy your sweet tooth.
Serving: Serves 4
Preparation Time: 5 minutes
Ready Time: 10 minutes

Ingredients:
• 2 cups of mixed berries (blueberries, blackberries, raspberries)
• 2 tablespoons of honey
• 2 teaspoons of fresh orange juice
• 2 vegitarian fresh peach, diced
• 1 teaspoon of fresh ginger, peeled and grated finely

- 2 cups of Greek yogurt
- 2 tablespoons of chopped pistachios

Instructions:
1. In a bowl, mix together the berries, honey, orange juice, diced peach, and grated ginger together.
2. Divide the mixture into 4 parfait glasses or dishes, layering it with the Greek yogurt.
3. Top each parfait with chopped pistachios.
4. Serve cold or at room temperature.

Nutrition information:
Calories: About 160 calories per serving; Fat: 2g; Carbs: 27g; Protein: 8g; Fiber: 3g; Sodium: 24mg.

18. Grilled Turkey Burgers

Grilled turkey burgers are an easy and delicious dinner option that can be enjoyed by the whole family. This recipe makes perfectly juicy and flavorful patties that are sure to be a hit!
Serving: 5 burgers
Preparation time: 10 minutes
Ready time: 25 minutes

Ingredients:
- 1 pound ground turkey
- 1/4 cup diced onion
- 1 teaspoon garlic powder
- 1 teaspoon dried oregano
- 1 teaspoon dried parsley
- Salt and pepper, to taste
- 5 burger buns
- Optional toppings: ketchup, lettuce, tomatoes, pickles

Instructions:
1. Preheat an outdoor grill or indoor grill pan to medium-high heat.
2. In a large bowl, combine the ground turkey, diced onion, garlic powder, oregano, parsley, and season with salt and pepper to taste.

3. Form the mixture into 5 equal-sized patties.
4. Place the patties on the preheated grill and cook for 4-6 minutes per side, or until the burgers are cooked through.
5. Toast the buns on the grill for 1-2 minutes, if desired.
6. Assemble the burgers on the buns with desired toppings and serve.

Nutrition information:
Calories: 261, Total Fat: 12 g, Saturated Fat: 3 g, Cholesterol: 90 mg, Sodium: 248 mg, Carbohydrates: 14 g, Fiber: 1 g, Sugar: 3 g, Protein: 24 g.

19. Beet and Carrot Salad

Beet and Carrot Salad is a fun and delicious salad that is made with raw beets and carrots, dressed in a lemon and dijon vinaigrette. Serve it as an accompaniment to your favorite main dish, or enjoy it as a light lunch or snack.
Serving: 4
Preparation time: 10 minutes
Ready time: 10 minutes

Ingredients:
-2 small beets, peeled and grated
-2 large carrots, peeled and grated
-2 tablespoons fresh lemon juice
-1 tablespoon dijon mustard
-2 tablespoons extra-virgin olive oil
-1/2 teaspoon sea salt
-2 tablespoons chopped chives, for garnish (optional)

Instructions:
1. In a large bowl, combine the grated beets and carrots.
2. In a separate bowl, whisk together the lemon juice, dijon mustard, olive oil, and sea salt.
3. Pour the dressing over the beet and carrot mixture and toss to combine.
4. Garnish with chopped chives, if using.
5. Serve immediately or chill in refrigerator until ready to serve.

Nutrition information:
Calories: 133
Fat: 8.5g
Carbohydrates: 13.7g
Protein: 2.4g
Fiber: 4.2g
Sugar: 7.8g

20. Baked Chicken Breast with Turmeric

Baked Chicken Breasts with Turmeric is a healthy and flavorful meal full of zesty flavor. The turmeric adds a unique and delicious flavor to the tender chicken breast. Serve with a side of rice or vegetables for a complete dinner.
Serving: 4
Preparation time: 10 minutes
Ready time: 40 minutes

Ingredients:
- 4 boneless, skinless chicken breasts
- 4 teaspoons olive oil
- 2 teaspoons garlic powder
- 1 teaspoon turmeric
- 1 teaspoon paprika
- 1 teaspoon onion powder
- Salt and black pepper, to taste

Instructions:
1. Preheat oven to 400 degrees F/200 degrees C.
2. Place chicken breasts in a large baking dish.
3. Drizzle olive oil over the chicken breasts and season with garlic powder, turmeric, paprika, onion powder, salt and black pepper.
4. Bake for 30-40 minutes, or until chicken is cooked through.
5. Serve immediately with your favorite side dish.

Nutrition information:

Calories: 249 kcal, Protein: 36 g, Fat: 10 g, Sodium: 208 mg, Fiber: 0 g, Carbohydrates: 0 g

21. Zucchini Noodles with Pesto

This zucchini noodles with pesto is an easy, healthy dish that combines spiralized zucchini "noodles" with a creamy pesto sauce. The combination of fresh basil, garlic, pine nuts, and parmesan cheese make this dish delicious and flavor-packed!
Serving: 2-4
Preparation Time: 15 minutes
Ready Time: 20 minutes

Ingredients:
- 2 zucchinis
- 2 tablespoons olive oil, plus extra for drizzling
- 2 cloves of garlic, minced
- 2 tablespoons pine nuts
- 2 tablespoons freshly grated parmesan cheese
- 1/4 teaspoon salt
- 1/8 teaspoon freshly ground black pepper
- 1/2 cup fresh basil leaves, lightly packed

Instructions:
1. Using a spiralizer, cut the zucchinis into "noodles".
2. Heat the 2 tablespoons of olive oil in a large skillet over medium heat.
3. Add the minced garlic and pine nuts and cook until fragrant.
4. Add the zucchini noodles to the skillet and cook until they are just tender, about 2 minutes.
5. In a food processor, combine the parmesan cheese, salt, pepper, basil, and remaining olive oil and blend until a creamy pesto consistency is formed.
6. Drizzle the pesto sauce over the zucchini noodles and toss to combine.
7. Serve with additional parmesan cheese, if desired.

Nutrition information:

Calories: 170, Total Fat: 14.2 g, Saturated Fat: 2.4 g, Cholesterol: 5.6 mg, Sodium: 135.9 mg, Total Carbohydrates: 7.2 g, Dietary Fiber: 2.1 g, Sugars: 3.5 g, Protein: 4.5 g

22. Ginger Turmeric Chicken Soup

This is a delicious and fragrant soup made by combining the aromatics of fresh ginger and turmeric with shredded cooked chicken. It's a healthy, hearty meal that can be enjoyed any time of the year!
Serving: 4-6
Preparation Time: 10 minutes
Ready Time: 25 minutes

Ingredients:
• 4-6 boneless, skinless chicken thighs
• 2 tablespoons vegetable oil
• 2 tablespoons fresh grated ginger
• 2 tablespoons fresh grated turmeric
• ½ teaspoon ground black pepper
• 2 cloves garlic, minced
• 5 cups chicken stock
• 1 large sweet potato, peeled and diced
• 1 teaspoon salt
• 2 tablespoons chopped fresh cilantro

Instructions:
1. Preheat the oven to 375°F.
2. Place the chicken thighs on a baking tray and roast for 25 minutes.
3. Heat the oil in a soup pot over medium heat.
4. Add the ginger, turmeric, pepper, and garlic and sauté until fragrant, about 2 minutes.
5. Add the chicken stock, sweet potato, and salt and bring to a boil.
6. Reduce the heat and simmer for 15 minutes.
7. Add the roasted chicken and simmer for 5 minutes.
8. Ladle the soup into individual bowls and top with cilantro.

Nutrition information:
Serving Size: 1 bowl

Calories: 200
Fat: 9g
Carbohydrates: 10g
Protein: 18g
Sodium: 670mg

23. Roasted Asparagus with Garlic

Roasted Asparagus with Garlic is a quick and easy side dish for an array of meals. This simple combination of asparagus, garlic, and olive oil will take any dinner to the next level.
Serving: Serves 4
Preparation time: 10 minutes
Ready time: 15 minutes

Ingredients:
• 2 pounds asparagus
• 1 tablespoon olive oil
• 2 cloves garlic, minced
• Salt and pepper, to taste

Instructions:
1. Preheat oven to 400 degrees.
2. Rinse and trim asparagus ends.
3. Place on baking sheet and drizzle with olive oil and garlic.
4. Sprinkle with salt and pepper.
5. Roast for 10 minutes, stirring once, or until tender and slightly golden.

Nutrition information:
• Calories: 103
• Fat: 7.4g
• Saturated Fat: 1.2g
• Sodium: 27mg
• Carbohydrates: 7.4g
• Fiber: 3.6g
• Protein: 4.3g

24. Mango Coconut Chia Pudding

Enjoy a delicious and healthy snack with this Mango Coconut Chia Pudding. A blend of mango, coconut, and chia seeds creates a nutrient-packed treat.
Serving: 2 servings
Preparation time: 10 minutes
Ready time: 2 hours

Ingredients:
- ½ cup frozen mango chunks
- ¼ cup canned coconut milk
- ¼ cup chia seeds
- ¼ teaspoon of coconut extract
- 2 drops of liquid stevia
- Pinch of salt

Instructions:
1. Place the mango chunks in a small bowl and microwave for 20 seconds on high power until melted.
2. In a medium bowl, whisk the coconut milk, chia seeds, coconut extract, liquid stevia, and salt until combined.
3. Pour the melted mango into the bowl with the other Ingredients. Stir to combine.
4. Place the bowl in the fridge and let sit for 2 hours until a pudding-like consistency is reached.

Nutrition information: Per serving: 168 calories; 10 g fat; 10 g carbohydrates; 5 g protein.

25. Spinach and Feta Stuffed Chicken Breast

The Spinach and Feta Stuffed Chicken Breast is an easy and delicious dish that makes for a perfect weeknight dinner.
Serving: 4
Preparation time: 10 minutes
Ready time: 40 minutes

Ingredients:
4 boneless, skinless chicken breasts
1 teaspoon olive oil
1/2 cup feta cheese, crumbled
1/3 cup cooked spinach, chopped
1/4 teaspoon dried oregano
1/8 teaspoon garlic powder

Instructions:
1. Preheat oven to 400°F.
2. On a cutting board, cut a pocket into each chicken breast.
3. In a bowl, mix together feta cheese, spinach, oregano, and garlic powder.
4. Stuff each chicken breast with the cheese and spinach mixture.
5. Place the chicken breasts in an oven-safe dish.
6. Drizzle with olive oil and season with salt and pepper.
7. Bake for 30-40 minutes or until chicken is cooked through.
8. Serve and enjoy.

Nutrition information: Per serving: Calories- 222, Protein- 27g, Carbohydrates- 6g, Fat- 9g, Sodium- 613mg

26. Quinoa and Black Bean Salad

This nutritious and delicious Quinoa and Black Bean Salad is sure to be a hit for any occasion! Paired with a bright and tangy homemade Citrus Vinaigrette, it's the perfect way to enjoy the flavors of the season.
Serving: 4
Preparation Time: 10 minutes
Ready Time: 10 minutes

Ingredients:
- 1/2 cup quinoa, cooked
- 1/2 cup black beans, rinsed and drained
- 1/4 cup red pepper, diced
- 1/4 cup green onion, diced
- 1/4 cup frozen corn
- 2 tablespoons fresh cilantro, chopped

- 2 tablespoons olive oil
- 2 tablespoons lime juice
- 1/4 teaspoon garlic powder
- Salt and pepper, to taste

Instructions:
1. In a medium bowl, combine the cooked quinoa with the black beans, red pepper, green onion, frozen corn, and fresh cilantro.
2. In a small bowl, whisk together the olive oil, lime juice, garlic powder, salt, and pepper. Drizzle the dressing over the salad and toss to combine.
3. Serve chilled or at room temperature.

Nutrition information:
Calories: 165 kcal, Carbohydrates: 18 g, Protein: 5 g, Fat: 9 g, Saturated Fat: 1 g, Sodium: 11 mg, Potassium: 213 mg, Fiber: 3 g, Sugar: 1 g, Vitamin A: 188 IU, Vitamin C: 12 mg, Calcium: 27 mg, Iron: 1 mg

27. Lemon Herb Baked Fish

This tasty Lemon Herb Baked Fish is a delicious bake for a family dinner. It only takes 35 minutes to prepare and cook, and is a hearty, flavorful meal!
Serving: Six
Preparation time: 15 minutes
Ready time: 25 minutes

Ingredients:
- 1/4 cup freshly squeezed lemon juice
- 2 teaspoons minced garlic
- 2 tablespoons olive oil
- 1 teaspoon dried oregano
- 1 teaspoon black pepper
- 1/4 teaspoon salt
- 1 1/2 pounds whitefish fillets (Cod, Tilapia, or Haddock)

Instructions:
1. Preheat oven to 350°F.

2. In a small bowl, combine lemon juice, garlic, olive oil, oregano, pepper, and salt, stirring until mixed.
3. Place fish fillets in a single layer in a greased baking dish.
4. Pour lemon mixture over the fish and place in preheated oven.
5. Bake for 15-20 minutes or until fish flakes easily with a fork.

Nutrition information:
Calories: 123, Fat: 5 g, Cholesterol: 54 mg, Sodium: 170 mg, Potassium: 399 mg, Carbohydrates: 1 g, Protein: 19 g

28. Cabbage and Carrot Slaw

This refreshing side dish combines crunchy cabbage and carrots with a zesty dressing, perfect for any occasion.
Serving: 6
Preparation Time: 10 minutes
Ready Time: 10 minutes

Ingredients:
1 head cabbage, cored and thinly sliced
2 carrots, shredded
1/4 cup olive oil
3 tablespoons white wine vinegar
1 teaspoon Dijon mustard
1 tablespoon honey
Salt and pepper to taste

Instructions:
1. In a large bowl, mix together the cabbage and the carrots.
2. In a separate bowl, whisk together the olive oil, white wine vinegar, Dijon mustard, and honey.
3. Pour the dressing over the cabbage and carrot mixture and stir to combine.
4. Season with salt and pepper to taste.
5. Refrigerate for at least 1 hour before serving.

Nutrition information: Nutrition per serving: Calories: 170; Fat: 11g; Saturated Fat: 1.5g; Cholesterol: 0mg; Sodium: 90mg; Carbs: 14g; Fiber: 4g; Sugar: 5g; Protein: 2g

29. Baked Turmeric Chicken Drumsticks

This delicious and healthy dish is perfect for a weeknight meal. Baked Turmeric Chicken Drumsticks are an easy and flavorful way to prepare chicken. They have a unique combination of lemon, garlic, and curry spices that will leave your taste buds tingling.
Serving
4-6
Preparation Time
10 minutes
Ready time: 30 minutes

Ingredients:
• 6-8 chicken drumsticks
• 2 tablespoons olive oil
• 2 tablespoons garlic, minced
• 2 tablespoons lemon juice
• 2 teaspoons turmeric
• 2 teaspoons curry powder
• 1 teaspoon garlic powder
• 1 teaspoon onion powder
• Salt and pepper to taste

Instructions:
1. Preheat the oven to 400F.
2. Place the drumsticks on a baking sheet lined with parchment paper and drizzle the olive oil over the drumsticks.
3. In a small bowl, mix together the garlic, lemon juice, turmeric, curry powder, garlic powder, onion powder, salt, and pepper.
4. Rub the mixture over the drumsticks until they are evenly coated.
5. Place the baking sheet in the preheated oven and bake for 25-30 minutes, or until the chicken is cooked through.
6. Remove the drumsticks from the oven and serve warm.

Nutrition information
Serving Size: 1 drumstick
Calories: 108
Protein: 11g
Fat: 7g
Carbohydrates: 2g
Sodium: 100mg

30. Green Smoothie with Kale and Pineapple

Green smoothies are a great way to pack a nutritional punch into one delicious drink. This one is a refreshing and energizing blend of kale and pineapple to really make you feel your best.
Serving: 1
Preparation Time: 5 minutes
Ready Time: 5 minutes

Ingredients:
• 1/2 cup kale
• 1/2 cup pineapple
• 1 peeled banana
• 1 cup cold coconut water
• 1/2 teaspoon chia seeds

Instructions:
1. Put the kale, pineapple, banana, and coconut water into a blender.
2. Blend until smooth.
3. Pour smoothie into a serving glass.
4. Sprinkle chia seeds over the top and stir together.

Nutrition information: Calories: 225, Protein: 5g, Carbs: 49g, Fat: 3g, Fiber: 12g.

31. Turmeric Roasted Potatoes

Turmeric Roasted Potatoes burst with flavor and are great as a side dish. Serve this delicious dish up with your favorite protein for a complete meal.

Serving: 4
Preparation Time: 10 minutes
Ready Time: 30 minutes

Ingredients:
- 4 to 5 small potatoes
- 2 tablespoons melted butter
- 1/4 teaspoon turmeric
- Salt and pepper

Instructions:
1. Preheat the oven to 400 degrees F.
2. Wash and scrub the potatoes. Cut them into bite-sized pieces.
3. Place the potatoes on a baking tray and drizzle the melted butter over them.
4. Sprinkle the turmeric, salt, and pepper over the potatoes and mix everything together.
5. Bake for 30 minutes or until potatoes are golden brown and tender.

Nutrition information:
- 182 calories
- 0 grams of fat
- 9 grams of carbohydrates
- 2 grams of protein

32. Grilled Shrimp and Vegetable Skewers

Grilled Shrimp and Vegetable Skewers is an easy and healthy meal that takes only 30 minutes to make. Its savory flavors of seafood and vegetables make the perfect accompaniment to any summer meal.

Serving: 4 servings
Preparation Time:10 minutes
Ready Time:20 minutes

Ingredients:

- 1 pound shrimp, peeled and deveined
- 1 bell pepper, cut into 1-inch cubes
- 2 tablespoons olive oil
- Salt and pepper, to taste
- 1/4 teaspoon paprika
- 1/4 teaspoon thyme
- 4 wooden or metal skewers

Instructions:

1. Preheat the grill to medium heat.
2. Toss together the shrimp, bell pepper, olive oil, salt, pepper, paprika, and thyme in a large bowl.
3. Thread the shrimp and pepper cubes onto the skewers, alternating between the two Ingredients.
4. Grease the grill with some oil and arrange the skewers on a heated grill.
5. Cook for 4-5 minutes on each side, or until the shrimp has turned a pink color and is cooked through.

Nutrition information: Each serving contains approximately 137 calories, 8g of fat, 2.05g of carbohydrates, and 13g of protein.

33. Cucumber and Avocado Gazpacho

This Cucumber and Avocado Gazpacho is a flavorful chilled soup that is the perfect summer appetizer. It takes only 10 minutes to prepare and is perfect for those hot days when you just don't want a hot soup.
Serving: 4
Preparation time: 10 minutes
Ready time: 10 minutes

Ingredients:

2 cucumbers, chopped
1 ripe avocado, pitted and chopped
1 small white onion, chopped
2 cloves of garlic, minced
1/2 cup cold water
2 tablespoons extra virgin olive oil

3 tablespoons white wine vinegar
1 lime, juiced
1 teaspoon honey
Kosher salt and freshly ground black pepper, to taste

Instructions:
1. In a high-speed blender, combine the cucumber, avocado, onion, garlic, cold water, olive oil, white wine vinegar, lime juice, honey, and season with salt and pepper to taste.
2. Blend until smooth, about 1 minute.
3. Taste and adjust seasonings as needed.
4. Refrigerate for at least an hour before serving.
5. Serve chilled in individual bowls.

Nutrition information:
Calories: 145 kcal, Carbohydrates: 11 g, Protein: 2 g, Fat: 11 g, Sodium: 7 mg, Potassium: 526 mg, Fiber: 5 g, Sugar: 4 g, Vitamin A: 221 IU, Vitamin C: 26 mg, Calcium: 35 mg, Iron: 1 mg

34. Spinach and Mushroom Quiche

Spinach and Mushroom Quiche is a hearty and flavorful dish made with a creamy egg custard, loaded with spinach, mushrooms, and cheese. It is a great choice for breakfast, lunch, or dinner.
Serving: 8-10
Preparation time: 15 minutes
Ready time: 45 minutes

Ingredients:
• 1 unbaked 9 inch pie crust
• 2 Tbsp butter
• 1 small onion, diced
• 2 cloves garlic, minced
• 1- 226 g package sliced mushrooms
• 2 cups fresh baby spinach, chopped
• 4 eggs
• 1/2 cup whole milk
• 1/2 cup heavy cream

- 1/4 tsp freshly ground nutmeg
- 1/2 tsp salt
- 1/4 tsp pepper
- 1/2 cup grated Parmesan cheese
- 1/2 cup shredded Gruyere cheese

Instructions:
1. Preheat the oven to 375°F. Place the pie crust in a 9 inch pie plate.
2. In a large skillet, melt butter over medium heat. Add onion and garlic and sauté for 3-4 minutes, until the onion is translucent. Add mushrooms and sauté for another 5 minutes. Add chopped spinach and continue to sauté for 2-3 minutes until the spinach has wilted.
3. In a large bowl, whisk together eggs, milk, cream, nutmeg, salt, and pepper. Stir in the Parmesan and Gruyere cheese. Add the sautéed mushroom and spinach mixture and stir to combine.
4. Pour the mixture into the prepared pie plate. Bake for 35-40 minutes, or until the custard has set and the top is golden brown. Allow to cool for 15 minutes before serving.

Nutrition information:
Per Serving (1/8):
Calories: 239, Fat: 15g, Saturated Fat: 7.5g, Cholesterol: 111mg, Sodium: 334mg, Carbohydrates: 16g, Fiber: 1.4g, Sugar: 3.2g, Protein: 12.1g

35. Baked Cod with Turmeric and Herbs

Baked Cod with Turmeric and Herbs is an easy and flavorful fish dish that is perfect for a quick weeknight dinner.
Serving: 4
Preparation time: 15 minutes
Ready time: 25 minutes

Ingredients:
- 4 cod fillets
- 4 tbsp olive oil
- 2 tsp garlic powder
- 2 tsp ground turmeric
- 2 tsp dried oregano

- 2 tsp dried basil
- 1 tsp thyme
- Salt and pepper to taste

Instructions:
1. Preheat the oven to 375 degrees F.
2. In a small bowl, combine the garlic powder, turmeric, oregano, basil, thyme, salt, and pepper.
3. Place the cod fillets in a shallow baking dish, making sure they are not overlapping.
4. Drizzle the top of the cod with olive oil, and then sprinkle generously with the herbal mixture.
5. Bake in the preheated oven for 15-20 minutes, until the cod easily flakes when pierced with a fork.

Nutrition information:
Calories: 212kcal, Carbohydrates: 1.g, Protein: 27g, Fat: 10.3g, Saturated Fat: 1.4g, Cholesterol: 58mg, Sodium: 147mg, Potassium: 340mg, Sugar: 0.1g, Vitamin A: 94IU, Vitamin B12: 0.8μg, Vitamin C: 1mg, Calcium: 15mg, Iron: 1.1mg.

36. Quinoa Stuffed Bell Peppers

Quinoa Stuffed Bell Peppers are a healthy and delicious meal that can be enjoyed for lunch or dinner. This plant-based meal is packed with nutrient-rich superfood Ingredients that will leave you satisfied and happy.
Serving: 4-6
Preparation time: 15 minutes
Ready Time: 45 minutes

Ingredients:
- 2 cups cooked quinoa
- 2 cups vegetable broth
- 6 medium bell peppers, cut in half and ribs & seeds removed
- 2 tablespoons olive oil
- 1 onion, minced
- 4 garlic cloves, minced

- 1/2 teaspoon dried oregano
- 1 teaspoon paprika
- 1 cup canned or cooked black beans
- 2 cups chopped fresh spinach
- 1/2 cup crumbled feta cheese
- Salt and pepper to taste

Instructions:
1. Preheat oven to 400°F.
2. In a large saucepan, heat the vegetable broth over medium-high heat. When the broth comes to a low boil, add the quinoa, cover, and reduce heat to low. Simmer for 15 minutes until most of the liquid has been absorbed. Fluff the quinoa with a fork and set aside to cool.
3. Meanwhile, heat the olive oil in a large skillet over medium-high heat. Add the onion and garlic and sauté for 3 minutes. Add the oregano, paprika, black beans, and spinach and cook for another 3 minutes until the vegetables are fragrant and the spinach has wilted.
4. Remove the skillet from heat and stir in the quinoa, feta cheese, and salt and pepper to taste.
5. Stuff each pepper with the quinoa filling and place in a greased baking dish. Bake for 25-30 minutes or until the peppers are tender.

Nutrition information (per serving):
Calories: 281
Fat: 8.9g
Carbohydrates: 40.2g
Protein: 11.2g
Fiber: 8.3g

37. Lemon Ginger Chicken Stir-Fry

 Lemon Ginger Chicken Stir-Fry is an easy and healthy stir-fry dish with a hint of sweetness that adds a great flavor. This refreshing dish is loaded with nutritious vegetables and fragrant aromatics and is perfect for a quick weeknight dinner.
Serving: Serves 4
Preparation Time: 10 minutes
Ready Time: 15 minutes

Ingredients:
- 2 tablespoons oil
- 1 pound boneless, skinless chicken breast, cut into thin strips
- 2 cloves garlic, minced
- 1 teaspoon freshly grated ginger
- 1 red bell pepper, thinly sliced
- 1 cup sliced mushrooms
- 1/3 cup chicken broth
- 2 tablespoons freshly squeezed lemon juice
- 1 teaspoon honey
- 1 teaspoon soy sauce
- 1 teaspoon cornstarch
- Salt and pepper, to taste
- 2 tablespoons chopped fresh Parsley

Instructions:
1. Heat the oil in a large skillet over medium-high heat. Add the chicken strips and cook for 3 minutes, or until lightly browned.
2. Add the garlic, ginger, bell pepper and mushrooms. Cook the vegetables for 3 minutes, or until lightly browned.
3. Add the chicken broth, lemon juice, honey, soy sauce and cornstarch to the skillet. Cook, stirring constantly, for 2 minutes, or until sauce thickens.
4. Season with salt and pepper, to taste. Sprinkle with parsley and serve.

Nutrition information: Calories: 268, Fat: 13 g, Carbohydrates: 13 g, Protein: 24 g, Sodium: 379 mg, Fiber: 4 g.

38. Roasted Beet and Goat Cheese Salad

A combination of sweet roasted beets and tangy goat cheese, this Roasted Beet and Goat Cheese Salad is an exciting meal! With a few simple Ingredients and some easy Instructions to follow, you can have a delicious salad in a matter of minutes.
Serving: Serves 4
Preparation time: 10 minutes
Ready time: 20 minutes

Ingredients:
- 4 beets, roasted
- 4 ounces goat cheese
- 4 tablespoons olive oil
- 2 tablespoons balsamic vinegar
- 2 tablespoons minced red onion
- 2 tablespoons fresh parsley
- Salt & pepper to taste

Instructions:
1. Preheat oven to 375 degrees.
2. Cut off the stems of the beets and wrap them in foil.
3. Roast in the oven for 45 minutes to an hour, or until fork tender.
4. Once roasted, let the beets cool. Peel and dice the beets into small cubes.
5. Place the beets in a large bowl and add the goat cheese, olive oil, balsamic vinegar, red onion, parsley, and salt & pepper to taste.
6. Gently toss until all Ingredients are well incorporated.
7. Serve immediately or refrigerate for up to 24 hours.

Nutrition information: (per serving) Calorie - 130, Total Fat - 8 g, Cholesterol - 12 mg, Sodium - 140 mg, Total Carbohydrates - 9 g, Protein - 6 g

39. Turmeric Coconut Curry Soup

This hearty Turmeric Coconut Curry Soup is packed with flavor thanks to the combination of red curry paste, coconut milk, and turmeric. The soup is both vegan and gluten-free.
Serving: 4
Preparation Time: 10 minutes
Ready Time: 20 minutes

Ingredients:
- 1 tablespoon olive oil
- 1 white onion, diced
- 4 cloves garlic, minced

- 2 tablespoons fresh ginger, grated
- 2 tablespoons red curry paste
- 1 teaspoon ground turmeric
- 1/2 teaspoon ground cayenne
- 4 cups vegetable broth
- 1 tablespoon maple syrup
- 1 can coconut milk
- 1 teaspoon sea salt
- 2 cups cooked quinoa or brown rice

Instructions:
1. Heat the olive oil in a large pot or Dutch oven over medium heat.
2. Add the onion and garlic and sauté for 4-5 minutes until lightly golden and fragrant.
3. Stir in the ginger, curry paste, turmeric, and cayenne and cook for 2 minutes.
4. Add the vegetable broth, maple syrup, and coconut milk and stir to combine.
5. Bring the soup to a simmer and cook for 10 minutes.
6. Add the cooked quinoa or brown rice and stir to combine.
7. Cook for an additional 3-4 minutes, until heated through.
8. Taste and adjust seasonings if desired.
9. Serve warm.

Nutrition information:
Calories: 268 kcal,
Carbohydrates: 29 g,
Protein: 10 g,
Fat: 12 g,
Saturated Fat: 6 g,
Sodium: 959 mg,
Potassium: 440 mg,
Fiber: 3 g,
Sugar: 4 g,
Vitamin A: 171 IU,
Vitamin C: 5 mg,
Calcium: 54 mg,
Iron: 2 mg

40. Roasted Garlic Cauliflower Mash

This roasted garlic cauliflower mash is a creamy and delicious side dish that's packed with flavor! It's an easy dish that can be prepared in under an hour and is both vegan-friendly and gluten-free.

Serving: 4-6
Preparation Time: 10 minutes
Ready Time: 45 minutes

Ingredients:
- 4 cloves of garlic, peeled
- 1 head of cauliflower, broken into florets
- 2 tablespoons of olive oil
- 2 tablespoons of vegan butter
- 1/2 cup of vegetable broth
- 1/4 teaspoon of salt
- 1/4 teaspoon of black pepper
- 2 tablespoons of chopped fresh parsley (optional)

Instructions:
1. Preheat the oven to 400 degrees Fahrenheit.
2. Place the garlic cloves and cauliflower florets on a baking sheet and drizzle with olive oil.
3. Roast the garlic and cauliflower for 25 minutes.
4. Meanwhile, melt the vegan butter in a medium saucepan over medium heat.
5. Once the butter is melted, add the vegetable broth and stir until combined.
6. Add the roasted garlic and cauliflower to the mixture and stir until combined.
7. Use an immersion blender or a potato masher to mash the Ingredients until creamy.
8. Add the salt and pepper and stir until combined.
9. Serve the roasted garlic cauliflower mash warm, topped with fresh parsley, if desired.

Nutrition information:
- Calories: 119
- Total Fat: 8.2 g
- Saturated Fat: 2.5 g

- Cholesterol: 0 mg
- Sodium: 281 mg
- Total Carbohydrates: 9.4 g
- Dietary Fiber: 2.8 g
- Sugars: 3.5 g
- Protein: 3.4 g

41. Berry Spinach Salad with Walnuts

This delicious Berry Spinach Salad with Walnuts is a perfect flavor combination of sweet and savory, making it a great light lunch or side salad.
Serving: 4-6
Preparation Time: 15 minutes
Ready Time: 15 minutes

Ingredients:
- 4 cups fresh spinach
- 2 cups sliced strawberries
- 2 cups blueberries
- ½ cup toasted walnuts
- 3 tablespoons olive oil
- 2 tablespoons balsamic vinegar
- 2 tablespoons honey
- Salt and pepper to taste

Instructions:
1. In a large bowl, combine spinach, strawberries and blueberries.
2. Toss the salad with the olive oil, balsamic vinegar, honey, salt and pepper.
3. Sprinkle the walnuts evenly over the salad and serve.

Nutrition information:
Calories: 163, Total Fat: 11.5g, Saturated Fat: 1.5g, Cholesterol: 0mg, Sodium: 70mg, Potassium: 256mg, Total Carbohydrates: 13.4g, Dietary Fiber: 2.4g, Sugars: 10g, protein: 3g.

42. Baked Turmeric Salmon with Herbs

This baked turmeric salmon with herbs is full of flavour and incredibly simple to make – perfect for weekday dinners.
Serving: Serves 4
Preparation Time: 15 minutes
Ready Time: 25 minutes

Ingredients:
- 4 salmon fillets
- 2 tablespoons olive oil
- 2 teaspoons ground turmeric
- 1 teaspoon garlic powder
- 4 tablespoons fresh chopped herbs (such as parsley, thyme, oregano, dill, etc.)
- Salt and pepper, to taste

Instructions:
1. Preheat oven to 375°F (190°C).
2. Grease a baking dish with olive oil.
3. Rub salmon fillets with olive oil and sprinkle with turmeric, garlic powder, herbs, and salt and pepper.
4. Place salmon fillets in the prepared baking dish and bake for 15 minutes or until cooked through.

Nutrition information:
Calories: 304 kcal, Carbohydrates: 1.1 g, Protein: 22.6 g, Fat: 23.2g, Sodium: 77 mg, Fiber: 0.4g, Sugar: 0 g

43. Quinoa and Vegetable Stir-Fry

This savory Quinoa and Vegetable Stir-Fry features a mix of hearty vegetables and flavorful quinoa for an easy and satisfying meal.
Serving: 4-5
Preparation time: 10 minutes
Ready time: 25 minutes

Ingredients:

- 1 cup uncooked quinoa
- 2 tbsp olive oil
- 1 onion, finely chopped
- 2 cloves garlic, minced
- 2 cups vegetables (such as carrots, bell pepper, and snow peas), roughly chopped
- 1/4 cup soy sauce
- 2 tsp brown sugar
- 1 tbsp sesame oil

Instructions:
1. Cook quinoa according to package Instructions. Set aside.
2. Heat the olive oil in a large skillet over medium-high heat.
3. Add onion and garlic and sauté until fragrant, about 2 minutes.
4. Add the vegetables and cook, stirring occasionally, until tender, about 10 minutes.
5. Add the cooked quinoa, soy sauce, and brown sugar. Cook, stirring occasionally, until everything is fully combined and heated through, about 3 minutes.
6. Stir in the sesame oil and serve.

Nutrition information: Serving size: 1/5 of the recipe | Cal: 294 | Total Fat: 9g | Saturated Fat: 1g | Cholesterol: 2mg | Sodium: 802mg | Carb: 39g | Fiber: 7g | Sugar: 5g | Protein: 7g

44. Lemon Garlic Herb Grilled Chicken

This juicy, fragrant lemon garlic herb grilled chicken is sure to be a crowd pleaser! It's an easy dish to make, and it's perfect for birthdays, celebratory meals, or just a regular weeknight dinner.
Serving: 6
Preparation time: 10 minutes
Ready time: 30 minutes

Ingredients:
- 2 lbs boneless, skinless chicken thighs
- 2 lemons, zested and juiced
- 6 cloves garlic, minced

- 2 tablespoons fresh thyme leaves
- 2 tablespoons fresh rosemary leaves
- 2 tablespoons olive oil
- 2 teaspoons kosher salt
- 1 teaspoon black pepper

Instructions:

1. In a small bowl, mix together garlic, thyme, rosemary, lemon zest, olive oil, salt, and pepper.
2. Place chicken thighs in a medium bowl and rub marinade into the chicken, covering all the pieces.
3. Heat a grill to medium high heat.
4. Place chicken thighs on the grill and cook, flipping once, until they reach an internal temperature of 165 degrees F, about 8-10 minutes per side.
5. While the chicken is grilling, mix together lemon juice and any remaining marinade in a small bowl.
6. Brush the lemon juice and marinade mix on the chicken, flipping once, until cooked through.
7. Serve with grilled lemon slices.

Nutrition information: Calories per serving: 213, Total Fat 9.3g, Saturated Fat 2.5g, Cholesterol 135mg, Sodium 522mg, Carbohydrates 4.3g, Fiber 0.7g, Protein 28.9g

45. Kale and Mango Smoothie

This Kale and Mango Smoothie is a nutritious and delicious smoothie that is perfect for a quick breakfast or snack.
Serving: Makes 2 servings
Preparation time: 5 minutes
Ready time: 5 minutes

Ingredients:
1 cup spinach or kale leaves
1/2 cup cubed mango
1/2 cup diced pear or peach
1 banana

1 cup non-dairy yogurt
1 cup almond milk

Instructions:
1. Put the spinach, mango, pear/peach, banana, yogurt, and almond milk in a blender.
2. Blend mixture until smooth.
3. Serve and Enjoy!

Nutrition information:
Calories: 194 kcal
Carbohydrates: 33.4 g
Protein: 7 g
Fat: 4.3 g

46. Ginger Turmeric Tofu Stir-Fry

Ginger Turmeric Tofu Stir-Fry is a quick and easy vegan meal packed full of flavour and fresh veggies. Perfect for a simple weeknight dinner.
Serving: 4
Preparation time: 15 minutes
Ready time: 25 minutes

Ingredients:
- 250g (1/2lb) of firm tofu, cubed
- 2 tablespoons of olive oil
- 2 cloves of garlic, minced
- 2 teaspoons of fresh ginger, grated
- 2 teaspoons of ground turmeric
- 1 red pepper, diced
- 2 carrots, sliced
- 2 spring onions/green onions, sliced
- 1/4 cup of soy sauce
- 2 tablespoons of maple syrup/honey
- 2 tablespoons of sesame seeds

Instructions:
1. Heat the olive oil over medium-high heat in a large skillet or wok.

2. Add the cubed tofu to the skillet and cook until golden brown, about 10 minutes.

3. Add the garlic, ginger, and turmeric to the skillet and cook for 1 minute.

4. Add the bell pepper, carrots, and spring onion to the skillet and cook for 5 minutes or until the vegetables are tender.

5. Add the soy sauce and maple syrup/honey to the skillet, and cook for 2 minutes.

6. Serve the stir-fry topped with sesame seeds.

Nutrition information: Calories: 219 kcal / Carbs: 17.1 g / Protein: 9.7 g / Fat: 14.5 g / Cholesterol: 0 g / Sodium: 613 mg / Sugar: 6.5 g

47. Roasted Brussels Sprouts and Quinoa Salad

This roasted Brussels sprouts and quinoa salad is an easy, protein-packed, and nutritious meal. It's a great way to add more flavor and texture to greens while getting lots of essential nutrients.
Serving: 4
Preparation time: 10 minutes
Ready time: 25 minutes

Ingredients:
-4 cups Brussels sprouts, halved
-2 tablespoons olive oil
-Salt and pepper to taste
-2 cups cooked quinoa
-1/4 cup almonds, sliced
-1/4 cup dried cranberries
-1/4 cup reduced-fat feta cheese

Instructions:
1. Preheat the oven to 400°F and line a baking sheet with parchment paper.
2. Place the Brussels sprouts on the baking sheet. Drizzle the Brussels sprouts with olive oil, salt, and pepper. Stir to combine, making sure the Brussels sprouts are evenly coated.

3. Roast the Brussels sprouts for 15-20 minutes, or until lightly golden and tender.

4. Remove the Brussels sprouts from the oven and place in a large bowl. Add the cooked quinoa, almonds, cranberries, and feta cheese to the bowl. Stir to combine.

5. Serve the roasted Brussels sprouts and quinoa salad warm or chilled.

Nutrition information:
Per 1/4 of the recipe : Calories: 218, Protein: 9 g, Fat: 10 g, Total Carbohydrate: 25 g, Dietary Fiber: 5 g, Sugar: 3 g

48. Lemon Dill Baked Cod

This Lemon Dill Baked Cod is a light and flavorful dish with the perfect balance of lemon, dill, and other seasonings. It's quick to prepare and requires minimal cleanup.

Serving: 4-6
Preparation Time: 15 minutes
Ready Time: 35 minutes

Ingredients:
- 2 lbs. cod filets
- 2 tablespoons olive oil
- 2 tablespoons lemon juice
- 2 tablespoons minced garlic
- 2 tablespoons chopped fresh dill
- Salt and black pepper to taste

Instructions:
1. Preheat oven to 400°F.
2. In a large bowl, whisk together olive oil, lemon juice, garlic, and dill.
3. Place cod filets in a lightly greased baking dish.
4. Pour olive oil mixture over the filets and season with salt and pepper.
5. Bake in preheated oven for 25 to 30 minutes or until the fish is cooked through and flaky.

Nutrition information: Per serving: 185 calories; 8.0 g fat; 5.1 g carbohydrates; 15.6 g protein; 64 mg cholesterol; 300 mg sodium.

49. Zucchini and Carrot Noodles with Pesto

This easy and delicious Zucchini and Carrot Noodles with Pesto dish is the perfect way to turn a few simple vegetables into an amazing weeknight meal.
Serving: 3-4
Preparation Time: 10 minutes
Ready Time: 10 minutes

Ingredients:
- 2 medium zucchinis, spiralized
- 1 medium carrot, spiralized
- 1/3 cup pesto
- 2 teaspoons olive oil

Instructions:
1. Heat olive oil in a large skillet over medium-high heat.
2. Add the zucchini noodles and carrot noodles to the skillet and cook for 2-3 minutes, stirring often.
3. Add pesto and combine until noodles are evenly coated.
4. Serve immediately.

Nutrition information:
Calories: 156
Carbs: 8 g
Protein: 4 g
Fat: 12 g
Sodium: 301 mg

50. Turmeric Lentil Soup

Turmeric Lentil Soup is a comforting and flavorful soup that is simple to make yet delivers a complex depth of flavor.
Serving: 4
Preparation Time: 10 minutes
Ready Time: 30 minutes

Ingredients:
- 2 tablespoons extra-virgin olive oil
- 2 cloves garlic, chopped
- 2 teaspoons ground turmeric
- 1 teaspoon ground cumin
- 1 medium onion, peeled and chopped
- 1 carrot, peeled and chopped
- 1 small red bell pepper, chopped
- sea salt and freshly ground black pepper, to taste
- 3 cups cooked lentils
- 8 cups vegetable broth
- 1/4 cup freshly chopped cilantro

Instructions:
1. Heat the olive oil in a large pot over medium heat.
2. Add the garlic, turmeric, and cumin to the pot and cook for 1 minute
3. Add the onion, carrot, bell pepper, sea salt and freshly ground black pepper and cook for 10 minutes, stirring occasionally.
4. Add the lentils, vegetable broth and bring to a boil.
5. Reduce to a simmer and cook for 20 minutes.
6. Once the soup is cooked, stir in the cilantro.
7. Serve the soup warm and enjoy!

Nutrition information: Calories: 315, Total Fat: 6g, Saturated Fat: 1g, Cholesterol: 0mg, Sodium: 797mg, Carbohydrates: 44g, Fiber: 19g, Sugar: 5g, Protein: 19g.

51. Roasted Garlic Mashed Sweet Potatoes

These Roasted Garlic Mashed Sweet Potatoes are a savory delight that are sure to become a family favorite! A delicious combination of roasted garlic, butter, and chives takes mashed sweet potatoes to a whole new level.
Serving: 8-10
Preparation Time: 15 minutes
Ready Time: 35 minutes

Ingredients:

- 4-6 sweet potatoes
- 6-8 cloves of garlic
- 2 tablespoons of olive oil
- 2 tablespoons of butter
- 1/4 cup of milk
- 2 tablespoons of chives
- Salt & pepper

Instructions:

1. Preheat your oven to 375°F.
2. Prepare the garlic: Peel the garlic cloves, then wrap them in aluminum foil with 1 tablespoon of olive oil, and a sprinkling of salt and pepper. Roast in the oven for 15 minutes. Set aside.
3. Peel and chop the sweet potatoes into 1 inch cubes and add them to a pot of boiling water. Cook for about 15 minutes until they are fork-tender. Drain and set aside.
4. In a medium-sized saucepan, melt the butter and remaining tablespoon of olive oil over medium-low heat, then add the roasted garlic cloves. Cook for 5 minutes, stirring occasionally, then add the cooked sweet potatoes.
5. Mash the potatoes and mix in the milk, chives, and additional salt and pepper to taste. Serve warm.

Nutrition information: (Per Serving, based on 10 servings)

- Calories: 123
- Fat: 8.4 g
- Carbohydrates: 14.5g
- Protein: 1.8g

52. Berry Chia Seed Smoothie Bowl

Start your day with this flavorful and nutritious Berry Chia Seed Smoothie Bowl. With the addition of chia seeds, this smoothie bowl provides an excellent source of omega-3 fatty acids and fiber.
Serving: 1 Serving: Preparation Time: 10 minutes
Ready Time: 10 minutes

Ingredients:

-1/2 cup frozen mixed berries (strawberries, blueberries, and raspberries)
-1 banana
-1/2 cup plain Greek yogurt
-1/4 cup almond milk
-1 tablespoon honey
-2 tablespoons chia seeds

Instructions:
1. In a blender, blend the frozen berries, banana, Greek yogurt, almond milk and honey until smooth.
2. Pour the smoothie into a bowl and top with chia seeds.
3. Serve immediately.

Nutrition information:
Calories: 330, Total fat: 9g, Saturated fat: 1.4g, Cholesterol: 3mg, Sodium: 78mg, Total carbohydrates: 49g, Dietary fiber: 9g, Sugars: 24g, Protein: 11g.

53. Turmeric Grilled Chicken Salad

Enjoy a delicious and healthy meal with this Turmeric Grilled Chicken Salad! This salad is loaded with succulent grilled chicken, fresh vegetables, and a zesty turmeric dressing.
Servings: 4
Preparation Time: 10 minutes
Ready Time: 20 minutes

Ingredients:
- 2 boneless skinless chicken breasts
- 1 teaspoon ground turmeric
- 2 tablespoons olive oil
- 1/4 teaspoon black pepper
- 1/2 teaspoon garlic powder
- 1/2 teaspoon onion powder
- 1 red pepper, sliced
- 1 cup cherry tomatoes, halved
- 1/2 cups cucumber, diced
- 1/2 cup red onion, diced

- 3 tablespoons fresh cilantro, chopped
- 2 tablespoons fresh lime juice

Instructions:
1. Preheat the grill to high heat.
2. Rub the chicken breasts with olive oil and sprinkle the turmeric, pepper, garlic powder, and onion powder over it.
3. Place the chicken on the grill and cook for about 8 minutes, flipping once, until cooked through.
4. Remove from the heat and let cool. Once cool, cut the chicken into cubes.
5. In a large bowl, combine the red pepper, tomatoes, cucumber, red onion, and cilantro.
6. Add the cubed chicken and toss with the fresh lime juice.
7. Plate the salad and serve.

Nutrition information:
Serving size: 1
Calories: 171 kcal
Fat: 8 g
Carbohydrates: 5 g
Protein: 22 g
Sodium: 31 mg
Fiber: 2 g

54. Quinoa and Black Bean Stuffed Bell Peppers

Quinoa and Black Bean Stuffed Bell Peppers is a hearty and satisfying dish that is full of flavour and nutrition.
Serving: 4
Preparation Time: 20 minutes
Ready Time: 50 minutes

Ingredients:
4 bell peppers of any color
1 cup quinoa
2 cups vegetable stock
1 can black beans

3 cloves of garlic, minced
1/4 cup diced onion
1/4 cup corn
4 tablespoons tomato paste
1 teaspoon chili powder
1 teaspoon oregano
Salt and pepper to taste

Instructions:
1. Preheat oven to 375°F (190°C). Cut the bell peppers in half, removing the tops, seeds, and stems.
2. In a medium-sized pot, combine the quinoa, vegetable stock, black beans, garlic, onion, and corn. Bring to a boil, then reduce heat to low and let simmer for 20 minutes.
3. Once quinoa is cooked through, mix in the tomato paste, chili powder, oregano, salt, and pepper.
4. Place the bell pepper halves in a baking dish. Stuff the peppers with the quinoa mixture and bake for 25 minutes.
5. Serve and enjoy!

Nutrition information: Each serving of Quinoa and Black Bean Stuffed Bell Peppers provides approximately 300 calories, 20g of protein, 45g of carbohydrates, and 6g of fat.

55. Lemon Garlic Shrimp Zoodles

Zucchini noodles diced up and sautéed with garlic, shrimps, and a delicate lemon sauce. This light and tasty Lemon Garlic Shrimp Zoodles dish will have you coming back for a second serving!
Serving: 4
Preparation Time: 10 minutes
Ready Time: 15 minutes

Ingredients:
- 4 Medium Zucchini/Courgette
- 2 tablespoons oil
- 4 cloves of garlic, finely diced
- 250g peeled and cooked small shrimp

- Juice from 1 lemon
- Salt and pepper to taste

Instructions:
1. Using a spiralizer (or knife if preferred) cut the zucchini/courgette into noodles.
2. Heat the oil in a large pan over medium heat.
3. Add the garlic and sauté for 1 minute.
4. Add the shrimp and cook for 2 minutes.
5. Add the lemon juice and season with salt and pepper to taste.
6. Add the zoodles to the pan and cook for 2-3 minutes, or until the zoodles are tender.
7. Serve immediately.

Nutrition information: Per serving: 180kcal, 2g fat, 10g carbohydrates, 23g protein.

56. Cabbage and Apple Slaw

Cabbage and Apple Slaw is a simple and healthy side dish that requires minimum Ingredients and effort. It is perfect for adding crunch and color to a variety of meals.
Serving: 4
Preparation time: 5 minutes
Ready time: 10 minutes

Ingredients:
• 2 cups finely shredded red cabbage
• 1 large apple, finely chopped
• 2 tablespoons freshly squeezed lemon juice
• 2 tablespoons extra-virgin olive oil
• 1 tablespoon honey or maple syrup
• 1/2 teaspoon ground black pepper
• 1/4 teaspoon fine sea salt

Instructions:
1. In a medium bowl, combine the cabbage and apple.

2. In a small bowl, whisk together the lemon juice, olive oil, honey, pepper, and salt.

3. Pour the dressing over the cabbage and apple mixture and toss until everything is evenly mixed.

4. Chill the cabbage and apple slaw in the refrigerator for 5 minutes prior to serving.

Nutrition information: Per Serving: 196 calories; 10.7 g fat; 24.3 g carbohydrates; 1.5 g protein; 3.2 g fiber

57. Baked Turmeric Chicken Thighs

This delicious dish combines the warm, nutty flavor of turmeric with the tender texture of roasted chicken thighs. Baked Turmeric Chicken Thighs is the perfect dinner or lunchtime meal for any occasion.
Serving: 4
Preparation time: 10 mins
Ready time: 45 mins

Ingredients:
•4 chicken thighs
•1 tablespoon olive oil
•1 teaspoon garlic powder
•1 teaspoon turmeric powder
•1 teaspoon smoked paprika
•Salt & pepper to taste

Instructions:
1. Preheat oven to 425 degrees F (220 degrees C).
2. In a large bowl, mix together olive oil, garlic powder, turmeric powder, smoked paprika, and salt & pepper.
3. Place chicken thighs into the bowl and mix to evenly coat them in the oil and spices mixture.
4. Place chicken thighs on a parchment paper lined baking sheet.
5. Bake for 20 minutes, then flip chicken thighs over and bake for an additional 25 minutes, or until chicken is cooked through.

Nutrition information: 4 servings, each with 497 kcal, 38.1g Fat, 21.2g Protein, 1.6g Carbohydrates, 0g Fiber.

58. Green Smoothie Bowl with Spinach and Banana

Start your day off right with this tasty and healthy Green Smoothie Bowl with Spinach and Banana. It's easy to make and loaded with beneficial antioxidants!
Serving: Makes 2 servings
Preparation Time: 5 minutes
Ready Time: 5 minutes

Ingredients:
- 1 banana
- 1 cup fresh spinach
- 1 cup almond milk
- 2 tablespoons chia seeds
- 2 tablespoons maple syrup (or to taste)

Instructions:
1. Place banana, spinach, almond milk, chia seeds, and maple syrup in blender.
2. Blend on high until a smooth and homogeneous mixture is achieved.
3. Divide the smoothie among two dishes and garnish with fresh fruit (or whatever desired toppings).
4. Serve and enjoy!

Nutrition information:
- Servings Size: 1 bowl
- Calories: 211
- Total Fat: 6.6g
- Cholesterol: 0.0mg
- Sodium: 84.3mg
- Total Carbohydrates: 33.7g
- Sugars: 16.8g
- Protein: 4.8g

59. Turmeric Roasted Cauliflower Steaks

Turmeric Roasted Cauliflower Steaks is an easy and flavorful preparation of an often overlooked vegetable. The savory, aromatic addition of turmeric, garlic and herbs make for a vibrant dish that is not only enjoyed as a main, but also as a side.
Serving: 4
Preparation time: 10 mins
Ready time: 25 mins

Ingredients:
- 1 large head of cauliflower
- 4 tablespoons olive oil
- 1 tablespoon garlic powder
- 1 teaspoon ground turmeric
- 1 teaspoon dried oregano
- 1 teaspoon paprika
- Salt and pepper, to taste

Instructions:
1. Preheat oven to 425 degrees F.
2. Cut the cauliflower into 4 thick steaks.
3. Mix olive oil, garlic powder, turmeric, oregano and paprika in a small bowl.
4. Using a brush, generously coat the cauliflower steaks with the seasonings mixture.
5. Place the steaks on a baking sheet lined with parchment paper.
6. Bake cauliflower steaks for 20 minutes, or until tender and golden.
7. Serve with your favorite sides.

Nutrition information: 67 calories, 9g carbohydrates, 3.5g fat, and 3g protein.

60. Lemon Herb Grilled Shrimp Skewers

Lemon Herb Grilled Shrimp Skewers are a quick and healthy way to grill a juicy, flavorful seafood dinner. The combination of lemon and herbs brings out the best in these succulent shrimp that can be cooked in a matter of minutes.

Serving: 4

Preparation Time: 15 minutes

Ready Time: 15 minutes

Ingredients:
- 1 pound large shrimp, deveined
- 2 tablespoons olive oil
- 2 teaspoons garlic powder
- 2 teaspoons dried oregano
- 2 tablespoons freshly squeezed lemon juice
- 1 tablespoon freshly chopped parsley
- Salt and freshly ground pepper to taste

Instructions:
1. Preheat the grill to medium-high heat.
2. In a bowl, combine the olive oil, garlic powder, oregano, lemon juice, parsley, salt, and pepper and whisk until combined.
3. Place the shrimp in the bowl and mix to fully coat with the marinade.
4. Thread the shrimp onto four skewers.
5. Grill the skewers for 2 minutes on each side or until the shrimp is cooked through.

Nutrition information:
Calories: 275 kcal, Carbohydrates: 2g, Protein: 34g, Fat: 14g, Saturated Fat: 2g, Cholesterol: 285mg, Sodium: 464mg, Potassium: 197mg, Fiber: 1g, Sugar: 1g, Vitamin A: 587IU, Vitamin C: 11mg, Calcium: 152mg, Iron: 3mg.

61. Cucumber Avocado Soup

This delicious Cucumber Avocado Soup is a cool and creamy vegan and paleo-friendly soup with a surprising flavor. It is best served on a hot summer day!

Serving: 6-8

Preparation time: 10 minutes

Ready time: 20 minutes

Ingredients:
- 2 avocados, ripe and diced
- 2 large cucumbers (about 2 pounds), peeled and diced
- 1/4 cup fresh lemon juice
- 1/4 cup extra-virgin olive oil
- 2 cloves garlic, minced
- 2 tablespoons fresh parsley, chopped
- 1 teaspoon sea salt
- 1/2 teaspoon black pepper
- 1/2 teaspoon ground cumin

Instructions:
1. In a blender or food processor, blend together the avocado, cucumbers, lemon juice, garlic, olive oil, sea salt, pepper and cumin until smooth.
2. Taste and adjust seasoning if necessary.
3. Divide soup into individual bowls and garnish with parsley.
4. Serve chilled.

Nutrition information: Per serving (based on 8 servings): Calories: 284, Protein: 3g, Fat: 20.5g, Carbohydrates: 25.7g, Fiber: 10.3g, Sugar: 6.1g, Sodium: 253.2mg

62. Spinach and Feta Stuffed Portobello Mushrooms

Spinach and feta stuffed portobello mushrooms are packed with flavor! Whole portobello mushroom caps are filled with a savory spinach and feta filling for a delectable vegetarian entree.
Serving: 6
Preparation Time: 15 minutes
Ready Time: 15 minutes

Ingredients:
• 6 portobello mushroom caps
• 1 tablespoon olive oil
• 2 cloves garlic, minced
• 2 cups baby spinach

- 1/4 teaspoon dried oregano
- 1/4 teaspoon dried basil
- Salt and pepper to taste
- 4 ounces feta cheese, crumbled

Instructions:
1. Preheat oven to 375 F. Line a baking sheet with foil and spray with cooking spray.
2. Clean portobellos with a damp paper towel and remove stems.
3. Place portobello caps stem-side down on the baking sheet. Bake for 10 minutes.
4. While the portobellos are baking, heat the olive oil in a large skillet over medium-high heat. Add garlic and cook until fragrant, about 30 seconds.
Add spinach and cook until wilted, about 2 minutes.
5. Remove from heat and stir in oregano, basil, salt and pepper.
6. Spoon the spinach mixture evenly into the portobellos and top each with feta cheese.
7. Bake for an additional 5 minutes, or until cheese is melted.

Nutrition information:
Calories: 167, Total Fat: 11.4g, Saturated Fat: 5.2g, Cholesterol: 25mg, Sodium: 335.8mg, Carbohydrates: 9.6g, Fiber: 2.3g, Sugar: 2.7g, Protein: 7.8g

63. Quinoa and Roasted Vegetable Salad

This salad combines roasted seasonal vegetables with cooked quinoa and a tasty vinaigrette dressing. It's a great way to enjoy a healthy and nutrient-rich meal in no time.
Serving: 4 servings
Preparation time: 10 minutes
Ready time: 25 minutes

Ingredients:
- 1 cup quinoa
- 1 red bell pepper, thinly sliced
- 1 small onion, thinly sliced

- 1 zucchini, cut into 1/2 inch slices
- 1 tablespoon olive oil
- Salt and pepper to taste
- 1/4 cup balsamic vinaigrette

Instructions:
1. Preheat oven to 375°F.
2. Spread quinoa, bell pepper, onion and zucchini on a greased baking sheet in a single layer.
3. Drizzle olive oil over the vegetables and season with salt and pepper.
4. Bake in preheated oven for 12-15 minutes or until vegetables are lightly browned and tender.
5. Remove from oven and allow to cool for 10 minutes.
6. In a large bowl, combine cooked quinoa, roasted vegetables and vinaigrette.
7. Serve immediately.

Nutrition information: Calories 212, Fat 10g, Protein 4.9g, Sodium 77.1mg, Carbohydrate 25.2g, Fiber 5.5g

64. Lemon Thyme Baked Fish

Serve up Lemon Thyme Baked Fish for your next meal! This fish dish is delicately seasoned with lemon juice and thyme leaves, cooked to perfection and served with a side of roasted vegetables and brown rice.
Serving: 4
Preparation Time: 15 minutes
Ready Time: 30 minutes

Ingredients:
- 4 fish fillets of your choice
- Juice of 1 lemon
- 2 tablespoons of butter
- 2 teaspoons of thyme leaves
- Salt and pepper to taste

Instructions:
1. Preheat oven to 375°F.

2. Place the fish fillets on a foil-lined baking sheet.

3. Pour the lemon juice over the fish.

4. Dot with butter and sprinkle with thyme leaves, salt and pepper.

5. Bake for 20-25 minutes until fish is cooked through.

6. Serve with roasted vegetables and brown rice.

Nutrition information:

Calories: 250 per Serving: Protein: 21g per serving

65. Ginger Turmeric Lentil Salad

This Ginger Turmeric Lentil Salad is easy to make, packed with flavor and has amazing health benefits! It's the perfect side dish or lunch for an easy vegan meal.

Serving: 4

Preparation Time: 10 minutes

Ready Time: 10 minutes

Ingredients:

- 1 cup brown or green lentils
- 2 tablespoons olive oil
- 1 teaspoon ground turmeric
- 1 teaspoon ground ginger
- 1 teaspoon ground cumin
- 1/2 teaspoon ground paprika
- 1/4 teaspoon sea salt
- 1 red onion, diced
- 2 carrots, grated
- 1 red bell pepper, diced
- 2 tablespoons freshly chopped parsley

Instructions:

1. Rinse the lentils in cold water and place them in a medium saucepan. Add enough water to cover the lentils by at least two inches and bring to a boil over high heat. Reduce the heat to medium-low and simmer, stirring occasionally, until the lentils are cooked through but still firm, about 10 minutes.

2. Meanwhile, heat the oil in a large skillet over medium heat. Add the turmeric, ginger, cumin, paprika, and salt and cook, stirring, for 1 minute. Add the onion, carrots, bell pepper and parsley and cook, stirring occasionally, for 3-4 minutes, until the vegetables are softened.
3. Remove the skillet from the heat and add the cooked lentils. Stir to combine, then transfer the lentil salad to a serving platter. Serve warm or cold.

Nutrition information:
Calories: 191 kcal | Carbohydrates: 26 g | Protein: 10 g | Fat: 5 g | Saturated Fat: 1 g | Sodium: 250 mg | Potassium: 528 mg | Fiber: 9 g | Sugar: 6 g | Vitamin A: 2760 IU | Vitamin C: 33 mg | Calcium: 53 mg | Iron: 4 mg

66. Roasted Garlic Brussels Sprouts and Quinoa

Roasted Garlic Brussels Sprouts and Quinoa is a delicious combination of roasted vegetables, quinoa, and garlic cooked to perfection. It is a great and savory dish that is perfect for weeknight dinners.
Serving: 4
Preparation time: 10 minutes
Ready time: 30 minutes

Ingredients:
-2 tablespoons olive oil
-1 lb Brussels sprouts, outer leaves discarded and sliced in half
-3 cloves garlic, minced
-1/2 teaspoon ground black pepper
-1/4 cup quinoa
-1/2 cup vegetable broth

Instructions:
1. Preheat oven to 375 degrees F.
2. In a large bowl, mix together olive oil, Brussels sprouts, garlic, and pepper. Spread out on a baking sheet.
3. Bake in preheated oven for 20-30 minutes, stirring occasionally.

4. In a saucepan, combine quinoa and vegetable broth. Bring to a boil, then reduce heat to medium-low. Cover and let simmer for 15 minutes or until quinoa is cooked.
5. Once both Brussels sprouts and quinoa are cooked, combine in a bowl and serve.

Nutrition information: Per serving: Calories: 162, Total fat: 6.6g, Saturated fat: 1.0g, Carbohydrates: 19.1g, Protein: 6.1g, Sodium: 60mg, Fiber: 4.4g

67. Mango Turmeric Smoothie

Start your day off with this delicious, sweet and fruity Mango Turmeric Smoothie! It's the perfect way to give your body a boost of antioxidants, healthy fats, fiber, and protein.
Serving: Makes 1 smoothie.
Preparation Time: 5 minutes
Ready Time: 5 minutes

Ingredients:
- ½ cup frozen mango
- 1 frozen banana
- ¼ teaspoon ground turmeric
- ¼ teaspoon cinnamon
- 1 teaspoon chia seeds
- ½ teaspoon ginger
- ¾ cup coconut milk
- Optional: 1 scoop of plant-based protein powder of choice

Instructions:
1. Place all of the Ingredients in a blender and blend until smooth.
2. Add more coconut milk or ice cubes if desired depending on desired consistency.
3. Serve immediately or store in refrigerator for up to 4 days.

Nutrition information: Calories: 210, Fat: 3.4 g, Carbohydrates: 39.7 g, Protein: 4 g, Fiber: 7.0 g, Sugar: 22.6 g

68. Turmeric Grilled Turkey Breast

Turmeric Grilled Turkey Breast is a simple yet flavorful recipe combining the earthy flavor of turmeric with juicy and smoky turkey. It's perfect for a simple weeknight dinner or as a main dish in a holiday spread.
Serving – Serves 4
Preparation Time - 10 minutes
Ready Time – 40 minutes

Ingredients:
–

2 lbs of boneless, skinless turkey breast
2 teaspoons turmeric
2 teaspoons grainy Dijon mustard
2 tablespoons olive oil
2 tablespoons honey
Salt and black pepper to taste

Instructions:
–

1. Preheat your grill to medium-high heat.
2. In a small bowl, whisk together the turmeric, mustard, olive oil, honey, salt, and pepper.
3. Rub the mixture all over the turkey breast and place it on the preheated grill.
4. Grill for about 20 minutes, flipping the turkey breast every 5 minutes.
5. Check the internal temperature of the turkey breast; the internal temperature should read 165°F.
6. Once cooked through, remove the turkey from the heat and let cool for a few minutes before slicing into thin strips.

Nutrition information - Calories: 285, Carbohydrates: 9.3g, Protein: 38.3g, Fat: 9.4g, Sodium: 112mg, Fiber: 0.3g

69. Zucchini Noodles with Lemon Garlic Shrimp

This delicious, light and refreshing dish of Zucchini Noodles with Lemon Garlic Shrimp is packed with flavor from the simple yet flavorful Ingredients.
Serving: Serves 4
Preparation Time: 10 minutes
Ready Time: 25 minutes

Ingredients:
- 4 medium zucchinis
- 1 lb. shrimp, peeled and deveined
- 2 tablespoons extra-virgin olive oil
- 2 cloves garlic, minced
- 2 tablespoons freshly squeezed lemon juice
- 2 tablespoons white wine
- 2 tablespoons chopped fresh parsley leaves
- Salt and freshly ground black pepper

Instructions:
1. Use a spiralizer to make the zucchini noodles. Place the zucchini noodles into a large bowl and set aside.
2. In a large skillet, heat the olive oil over medium-high heat. Add the garlic and cook until lightly golden, about 30 seconds.
3. Add the shrimp and season with salt and pepper. Cook until the shrimp are just cooked through, about 3 minutes.
4. Add the lemon juice, white wine and fresh parsley. Cook for about 1 minute.
5. Toss the zucchini noodles with the shrimp mixture. Cook for about 2 minutes.
6. Serve warm.

Nutrition information: (per serving) Calories: 213; Protein: 23.6g; Fat: 9.2g; Carbohydrates: 6.6g; Fiber: 2.4g; Sugars: 3g; Sodium: 345mg.

70. Beet and Quinoa Salad with Citrus Dressing

This is a fresh and vibrant salad that combines the earthy flavors from beets, the crunch from quinoa and the citrus flavors from a tangy lemon dressing.

Serving: Serves 4
Preparation time: 10 minutes
Ready time: 10 minutes

Ingredients:
- 2 cups cooked beets, cubed
- 1 cup uncooked quinoa
- 2 oranges, peeled and segments removed
- 1/2 cup feta cheese
- 2 tablespoons olive oil
- Juice of 2 lemons
- 2 cloves garlic, minced
- 2 tablespoons fresh parsley, minced
- 1 teaspoon fresh oregano, minced
- Salt and pepper, to taste

Instructions:
1. Cook the quinoa according to the directions on the package.
2. In a large bowl, combine cooked quinoa, cubed beets, orange segments and feta cheese.
3. In a Mason jar, combine olive oil, lemon juice, garlic, parsley and oregano. Shake to combine.
4. Pour dressing over salad and toss to coat. Season with salt and pepper.
5. Serve immediately.

Nutrition information:
Calories per serving: 238; Protein: 8 g; Total fat: 12 g; Sodium: 109 mg; Total carbohydrates: 26 g; Dietary fiber: 5 g; Sugars: 9 g; Cholesterol: 16 mg.

71. Lemon Garlic Herb Baked Salmon

This dish combines fresh lemon, garlic, and herbs to give succulent baked salmon a savory flavor. It's an easy dish to make with minimal Ingredients yet maximum flavor.

Serving: Serves 4 people.
Preparation time: 10 minutes.
Ready time: 30 minutes.

Ingredients:
• 4 salmon fillets
• 2 tablespoons olive oil
• 1/4 cup lemon juice
• 2 tablespoons minced garlic
• 2 tablespoons minced parsley
• 2 tablespoons minced oregano
• Salt and freshly ground pepper, to taste

Instructions:
1. Preheat oven to 350°F (177°C).
2. Arrange the salmon fillets on a greased baking sheet.
3. In a small bowl, combine the olive oil, lemon juice, garlic, parsley and oregano.
4. Pour the mixture over the salmon, and season with salt and pepper.
5. Bake in the preheated oven for 25-30 minutes, until the salmon is cooked through and flakes easily with a fork.

Nutrition information
Calories: 280kcal, Carbohydrates: 2g, Protein: 25g, Fat: 17g, Saturated Fat: 3g, Cholesterol: 66mg, Sodium: 132mg, Potassium: 575mg, Fiber: 1g, Sugar: 1g, Vitamin A: 79IU, Vitamin C: 8mg, Calcium: 38mg, Iron: 2mg

72. Ginger Turmeric Chickpea Stir-Fry

This Ginger Turmeric Chickpea Stir-Fry dish is a flavorful and easy-to-make vegan dish. It is packed with nutrition, and great for a quick lunch or dinner.
Serving: 4
Preparation Time: 10 minutes
Ready Time: 25 minutes

Ingredients:
1 tsp coconut oil

1 onion, diced
3 cloves garlic, minced
2 tbsp freshly grated ginger root
1 tsp ground turmeric
1 can Chickpeas, drained and rinsed
1 bell pepper, diced
1/4 cup vegetable broth
1/4 cup chopped fresh cilantro
Salt & pepper, to taste

Instructions:
1. Heat a large skillet over medium-high heat.
2. Add the coconut oil and onion and cook for 4 minutes, stirring occasionally.
3. Add the garlic, ginger, and turmeric and cook for an additional 2 minutes, stirring constantly.
4. Add the chickpeas, bell pepper, and vegetable broth and cook for 10-12 minutes, stirring occasionally.
5. Remove from heat and add the cilantro, salt and pepper and stir to combine.

Nutrition information: (Per Serving)
Calories: 142
Fat: 4.7g
Saturated Fat: 3.6g
Carbohydrates: 20g
Fiber: 7.2g
Protein: 6g
Sugar: 4.2g

73. Roasted Butternut Squash and Kale Salad

Roasted Butternut Squash and Kale Salad is a hearty and flavorful vegan salad, that is packed with flavor, nutrition and texture.
Serving: 4-6
Preparation Time: 15 minutes
Ready Time: 45 minutes

Ingredients:
- -1 butternut squash, peeled, seeded and cut into ½" cubes
- -1 tablespoon olive oil
- -1 teaspoon kosher salt
- -1 teaspoon pepper
- -3 cups chopped kale
- -1/4 cup thinly sliced red onion
- -1/4 cup pine nuts
- -1/4 cup golden raisins
- -3 tablespoons balsamic vinegar
- -2 tablespoons extra virgin olive oil
- -1/2 teaspoon honey

Instructions:
1. Preheat oven to 400° F.
2. Place butternut squash cubes on a baking sheet and drizzle with olive oil. Sprinkle with salt and pepper and toss to combine.
3. Bake in the oven for 25-30 minutes, stirring once.
4. Remove from oven and let cool for a few minutes.
5. In a large bowl, combine the kale, red onion, and pinenuts.
6. In a small bowl, whisk together the balsamic vinegar, olive oil, and honey.
7. Pour the dressing over the kale mixture and toss to combine.
8. Add the roasted butternut squash and golden raisins and toss to combine.
9. Serve.

Nutrition information: Serving Size: 1/6 of recipe | Calories: 200 | Total Fat: 12g | Saturated Fat: 2g | Trans Fat: 0g | Cholesterol: 0mg | Sodium: 190mg | Total Carbohydrate: 22g | Dietary Fiber: 4g | Total Sugars: 8g | Protein: 4g

74. Turmeric Coconut Lentil Curry

This creamy Turmeric Coconut Lentil Curry is a delicious vegan dish that's easy to prepare and just as flavorful as more time-consuming recipes. With a handful of simple Ingredients and minimal kitchen time, you can have a warm, comforting dinner in no time.

Serving: Serves 4
Preparation time: 15 minutes
Ready time: 30 minutes

Ingredients:
- 2 tablespoons coconut oil
- 1 cup uncooked red lentils, rinsed
- 1 yellow onion, diced
- 1 tablespoon minced garlic
- 2 ¼ teaspoon ground turmeric
- 1 teaspoon ground cumin
- 1 (14oz) can of coconut milk
- 1 ½ cups low-sodium vegetable broth
- 1 teaspoon sea salt
- 2 tablespoons lime juice

Instructions:
1. Heat the coconut oil in a large 4-quart soup pot.
2. Add in the onion, garlic and turmeric, cook until the onion is softened and fragrant, about 5 minutes.
3. Add in the lentils, cumin, coconut milk, vegetable broth, and salt.
4. Bring the mixture to a boil, then reduce to heat to low simmer.
5. Simmer uncovered for about 20 minutes, stirring occasionally, until the lentils are tender.
6. Stir in the lime juice.
7. Serve hot with steamed rice or naan.

Nutrition information: Per Serving - 428 Calories, 17g Protein, 25g Fat,

75. Roasted Garlic Mashed Cauliflower

Roasted Garlic Mashed Cauliflower is a flavorful and healthy side dish that's packed full of tons of nutrients. Creamy and super tasty, it's a great alternative to traditional mashed potatoes.
Serving: 4-6
Preparation time: 10 minutes
Ready time: 35 minutes

Ingredients:
- 2 tablespoons olive oil
- 2 heads of cauliflower, divided into florets
- 3-4 cloves roasted garlic
- 1/4 cup non-dairy milk
- 1/4 cup freshly grated Parmesan
- Salt and freshly ground black pepper to taste
- 2 tablespoons fresh parsley, chopped

Instructions:
1. Preheat oven to 430 degrees F (220 degrees C).
2. Place the cauliflower florets on a baking sheet and drizzle olive oil over them. Toss to coat.
3. Roast for 25 minutes or until crispy on the outside and soft on the inside.
4. Place the roasted cauliflower in a food processor and add the roasted garlic. Blend until creamy and smooth.
5. Add the non-dairy milk, Parmesan, salt, and pepper. Blend again until creamy and smooth.
6. Pour the mashed cauliflower into a serving bowl and garnish with parsley. Serve immediately.

Nutrition information: Per Serving: 125 calories, 4.3g fat, 17g carbohydrates, 5.5g protein, 3.3g fiber

76. Mixed Berry Spinach Smoothie

Beat the mid-week slump with this delicious Mixed Berry Spinach Smoothie! This powerhouse smoothie is packed with antioxidants, vitamin C, iron, calcium, and so much more.
Serving: 2
Preparation Time: 10 minutes
Ready In: 10 minutes

Ingredients:
• 1 cup fresh spinach
• 1 cup frozen mixed berries

- 1 banana
- 1 cup low-fat milk
- 2 tablespoons honey

Instructions:
1. In a blender, add spinach, berries, banana, milk, and honey.
2. Blend until all Ingredients are smooth.
3. Divide smoothie into two glasses.
4. Enjoy!

Nutrition information:
- Calories: 175
- Fat: 2g
- Sodium: 79mg
- Carbohydrates: 38g
- Protein: 5g

77. Turmeric Grilled Vegetable Skewers

Enjoy the wonderful flavors of turmeric and grilled vegetables with these delicious turmeric grilled vegetable skewers! Serve as a side dish or as an entree.
Serving: 4
Preparation time: 15 minutes
Ready time: 20 minutes

Ingredients:
- 2 large zucchini, cut into cubes
- 2 large bell peppers, cut into cubes
- 1 large onion, cut into cubes
- 2 tablespoons olive oil
- 2 teaspoons ground turmeric
- Salt and pepper to taste

Instructions:
1. Preheat the grill to medium-high heat.
2. In a large bowl, combine the zucchini, bell peppers, and onion.
3. Add the olive oil, ground turmeric, and salt and pepper and mix well.

4. Skewer the vegetables on skewers and place on the preheated grill.
5. Grill for 15-20 minutes or until vegetables are tender and lightly browned.
6. Serve warm.

Nutrition information: Per Serving - Calories: 121; Fat: 7g; Carbohydrates: 11g; Protein: 2g; Fiber: 3g

78. Cucumber Avocado Quinoa Salad

Try this delicious and protein-packed Cucumber Avocado Quinoa Salad – it's an easy side dish that's sure to become a new favorite in your house!
Serving: 4-6
Preparation Time: 15 minutes
Ready Time: 15 minutes

Ingredients:
• 1 cup uncooked quinoa
• 2 cups vegetable broth
• 1 cup cherry tomatoes, halved
• 1/2 English cucumber, chopped
• 1 large avocado, chopped
• Juice of 1 lemon
• 2 tablespoons olive oil
• 2 tablespoons fresh basil, chopped
• Sea salt and freshly ground black pepper, to taste

Instructions:
1. In a medium pot, cook the quinoa with vegetable broth until all liquid has been absorbed, about 15 minutes.
2. Transfer the cooked quinoa to a bowl and let it cool for 15 minutes.
3. Once cool, stir in cherry tomatoes, cucumber and avocado.
4. In a small bowl, whisk together lemon juice, olive oil, and basil. Season with salt and pepper, to taste.
5. Drizzle the dressing over the salad and toss to combine.

Nutrition information: (Per Serving)Calories: 261, Protein: 6g, Fat: 11.1g, Carbs: 32.1g, Fiber: 8.2g, Sugar: 3.6g

79. Lemon Herb Grilled Chicken Thighs

This Lemon Herb Grilled Chicken Thighs recipe is a perfect dish to make for a weeknight or special occasion. The marinade adds an extra layer of flavor to the chicken with the combination of lemon, herbs, and spices, making it a delicious and versatile meal.

Serving: 6
Preparation time: 10 minutes
Ready time: 30 minutes

Ingredients:
- 8 chicken thighs
- 2 cloves of garlic (minced)
- 2 tablespoons lemon juice
- 2 tablespoons olive oil
- 2 tablespoons chopped fresh herbs, such as thyme, rosemary, and oregano
- 2 tablespoons Dijon mustard
- 1 teaspoon freshly cracked black pepper
- Salt to taste

Instructions:
1. In a large bowl, combine the garlic, lemon juice, olive oil, herbs, Dijon mustard, and black pepper. Whisk together until all the Ingredients are combined.
2. Add the chicken thighs to the bowl and turn to coat evenly. Cover and let the chicken marinate for at least 15 minutes, or refrigerate overnight for best results.
3. Preheat grill to medium-high heat.
4. Remove the chicken from the marinade and discard marinade. Place the chicken on the grill and cook for about 10 minutes on each side, flipping once, until the chicken is cooked through and the juices run clear.

Nutrition information:

Serving size: 1 chicken thigh • Calories: 180 • Fat: 7.5g • Carbs: 0.6g • Protein: 25.3g

80. Ginger Turmeric Tofu and Vegetable Stir-Fry

This delicious Ginger Turmeric Tofu and Vegetable Stir-Fry is a quick and easy weeknight dinner that packs a punch with bold flavors and nutritious Ingredients.
Serving: Serves 4
Preparation time: 10 minutes
Ready time: 25 minutes

Ingredients:
- 2 tablespoons olive oil
- 1 red onion, chopped
- 1 large garlic clove, minced
- 2 tablespoons freshly grated ginger
- 1 tablespoon ground turmeric
- 12 ounces extra-firm tofu, cut into ½-inch cubes
- 2 cups roughly chopped vegetables of your choice
- 2 tablespoons tamari
- 1 teaspoon sesame oil
- 3 tablespoons cashews, chopped

Instructions:
1. Heat olive oil in a large deep skillet over medium heat.
2. Add red onion and garlic and cook until soft.
3. Add ginger and turmeric and continue stirring for another few seconds.
4. Add tofu and vegetables and cook until vegetables are tender.
5. Add tamari and sesame oil and stir to combine.
6. Stir in cashews and cook for a few more minutes.
7. Serve hot.

Nutrition information: Per serving: 279 Calories; 18g Fat; 15g Protein; 13g Carbohydrate; 5g Dietary Fiber; 810mg Sodium.

81. Roasted Beet and Quinoa Salad with Feta

Roasted Beet and Quinoa Salad with Feta is a delicious and healthy dish combining roasted beets, quinoa and feta, along with other Ingredients to create a flavorful and fresh salad.

Serving: 4

Preparation time: 10 minutes

Ready time: 50 minutes

Ingredients:
- 4 medium beets
- 1 cup quinoa
- ¼ cup olive oil
- 1 tablespoon minced garlic
- ¼ teaspoon black pepper
- ¼ teaspoon red pepper flakes
- ¼ cup white vinegar
- 2 tablespoons lemon juice
- ¼ cup minced red onion
- 2 tablespoons chopped fresh parsley
- ¼ cup crumbled feta cheese

Instructions:
1. Preheat your oven to 375°F.
2. Peel and cut the beets into small cubes. Place them on a parchment-lined baking sheet.
3. Drizzle with 2 tablespoons olive oil and a pinch of salt. Mix to coat.
4. Roast for 20-25 minutes, or until beets are fork tender.
5. While your beets are roasting, cook the quinoa according to package Instructions.
6. In a small bowl, whisk together the remaining ¼ cup olive oil, garlic, black pepper, red pepper flakes, white vinegar, and lemon juice.
7. When the beets and quinoa are done, combine in a large bowl.
8. Add the dressing, red onion, parsley, and feta cheese.
9. Gently toss the salad together until all the Ingredients are evenly distributed.
10. Serve warm or chilled.

Nutrition information: Calories- 270, Total Fat-14g (Saturated Fat-3g), Cholesterol- 6mg, Sodium- 232mg, Total Carbohydrates- 28g, Dietary Fiber- 4g, Sugar- 8g, Protein- 7g

82. Lemon Garlic Baked Cod

Try this delicious and easy Lemon Garlic Baked Cod recipe for a quick mid-week dinner.
Serving: 4
Preparation time: 5 minutes
Ready time: 20 minutes

Ingredients:
• 4 cod fillets
• 1 teaspoon garlic powder
• 2 tablespoons olive oil
• 2 lemons, zested
• 2 tablespoons fresh parsley, chopped

Instructions:
1. Preheat oven to 375 degrees.
2. In a small bowl, mix together garlic powder, olive oil, lemon zest, and parsley.
3. Place cod fillets on a lined baking sheet.
4. Rub the olive oil mixture on top of the fish.
5. Bake for 20 minutes.

Nutrition information:
• Calories: 160
• Total Fat: 6g
• Sodium: 251mg
• Carbohydrates: 4g
• Protein: 21g

83. Zucchini Noodles with Turmeric Pesto

Zucchini noodles with Turmeric Pesto is a creamy, flavorful and healthy dish that is made with pesto, zucchini, pine nuts, and turmeric. The combination of all the Ingredients makes for a nutritious and delicious meal.

Serving: 4
Preparation time: 10 minutes
Ready time: 15 minutes

Ingredients:
- 2 medium-sized zucchini
- 2 tablespoons pine nuts
- 1 garlic clove, minced
- 2 tablespoons olive oil
- 2 tablespoons lemon juice
- 2 tablespoons freshly chopped parsley
- 1 teaspoon of salt
- 1 teaspoon ground turmeric
- ¼ teaspoon of freshly ground black pepper

Instructions:
1. Use a spiralizer to create zucchini noodles, or use a vegetable peeler to create thin strips of the zucchini.
2. To make the pesto, combine the pine nuts, garlic, olive oil, lemon juice, parsley, salt, turmeric and black pepper in a food processor and blend until smooth.
3. Place the zucchini noodles into a large bowl and pour the pesto over them. Toss the noodles to coat in the pesto.
4. Heat a large skillet over medium-high heat and cook the zucchini noodles for 5-7 minutes, stirring occasionally.
5. Serve the noodles hot with additional lemon juice and parsley.

Nutrition information:
160 calories, 12.6 grams of fat, 5.9 grams of carbohydrates, 2.9 grams of protein, and 0.2 grams of fiber in each serving.

84. Turmeric Lentil Stew

This comforting and flavorful Turmeric Lentil Stew is the perfect meal for those cold winter nights. It has a mild taste and is loaded with plant-based protein.

Serving: 4-6
Preparation Time: 15 minutes
Ready Time: 30 minutes

Ingredients:
- 1 tablespoon olive oil
- 1 small onion, diced
- 2 cloves garlic, minced
- 2 carrots, diced
- 1 teaspoon ground turmeric
- 1 teaspoon ground cumin
- 1 teaspoon ground coriander
- 2 cups uncooked red lentils
- 4 cups vegetable broth
- Salt and pepper to taste

Instructions:
1. Heat olive oil in a large saucepan over medium heat.
2. Add onion and garlic, and cook until softened, about 5 minutes.
3. Add carrots, turmeric, cumin, and coriander, and cook for an additional 2 minutes.
4. Add lentils and vegetable broth, and bring to a boil.
5. Reduce heat to a simmer, and cook for 20 minutes, or until lentils are tender.
6. Season with salt and pepper to taste.

Nutrition information: Per Serving (Based on 6 servings): Calories: 160, Total Fat: 2.6 g, Saturated Fat: 0.4 g, Cholesterol: 0 mg, Sodium: 819 mg, Total Carbohydrate: 27.8 g, Dietary Fiber: 9 g, Sugars: 5.4 g, Protein: 9.7 g

85. Roasted Garlic Mashed Potatoes

Roasted Garlic Mashed Potatoes are a delicious side dish, made with roasted garlic that gives the mashed potatoes a unique flavor.

Serving: 6
Preparation Time: 15 minutes
Ready Time: 40 minutes

Ingredients:
-4 cloves garlic
-3 pounds russet potatoes, peeled and quartered
-½ cup unsalted butter
-1 cup half-and-half
-½ cup grated Parmesan cheese
-1 tablespoons chopped fresh chives
-2 teaspoons salt
-1 teaspoon freshly ground pepper

Instructions:
1. Preheat oven to 375°F.
2. Place garlic cloves onto a sheet of foil and wrap up.
3. Place in the preheated oven and roast for 25 minutes.
4. Meanwhile, place potatoes in a large pot filled with enough water to cover and bring to a boil over high heat.
5. Reduce heat to medium-low and simmer for 15 minutes or until potatoes are tender.
6. Drain the potatoes and then return them to the pot.
7. Mash potatoes with a potato masher.
8. Unwrap the garlic and add it to the mashed potatoes.
9. Add butter, half-and-half, Parmesan cheese, chives, salt, and pepper and mash until creamy.

Nutrition information: Per serving: 339 calories, 21 g fat, 2g protein, 28g carbohydrate, 2g fiber, 1g sugar, 66mg sodium.

86. Berry Spinach Smoothie Bowl

Start the day off right with this comforting Berry Spinach Smoothie Bowl, an easy-to-make, nutritious breakfast.
Serving: 2
Preparation time: 5 minutes
Ready time: 5 minutes

Ingredients:
- ⬛1 cup fresh spinach
- ¾ cup frozen strawberries
- ½ cup frozen blueberries
- ½ banana
- 1/4 to 1/2 cup water
- 1 teaspoon honey
- ½ teaspoon vanilla extract
- ¼ cup chopped almonds (or nuts of choice)
- ¼ cup goji berries
- 2 tablespoons shredded coconut

Instructions:
1. Combine the spinach, strawberries, blueberries, banana, honey, water, and vanilla extract together in a blender.
2. Blend until smooth and creamy.
3. Divide between two serving bowls.
4. Top each with the almonds, goji berries, and shredded coconut.
5. Serve immediately.

Nutrition information:
Calories: 249 | Carbohydrates: 29g | Protein: 5g | Fat: 13g | Sodium: 43mg | Sugar: 18g | Fiber: 6g

87. Turmeric Grilled Salmon with Herbs

This Turmeric Grilled Salmon with Herbs recipe is a flavorful and delicious dinner option that takes less than 30 minutes to make.
Serving: Serves 4
Preparation Time: 5 minutes
Ready Time: 25 minutes

Ingredients:
- 4 (6-ounce) salmon fillets
- 1 teaspoon ground turmeric
- 2 tablespoons olive oil
- Salt and pepper, to taste

- 2 tablespoons fresh herbs (such as parsley, basil, thyme), chopped

Instructions:
1. Preheat the grill over medium-high heat.
2. Pat the salmon dry with a paper towel and season one side with turmeric, olive oil, salt, and pepper.
3. Place the salmon on the preheated grill with the seasoned side down and cook for 5 minutes.
4. Flip the salmon over and cook for 3-4 more minutes, or until desired doneness.
5. Remove from heat and sprinkle with fresh herbs.

Nutrition information: Calories: 279, Fat: 14.5g, Saturated Fat: 2.3g, Cholesterol: 94mg, Sodium: 89mg, Carbohydrates: 0.8g, Fiber: 0.4g, Protein: 32.2g

88. Quinoa and Chickpea Stir-Fry

Quinoa and chickpea stir-fry is an easy and nutritious vegan dish made with cooked quinoa, chickpeas and vegetables. It is flavorful with just the right amount of spice, ready to enjoy in under 30 minutes.
Serving: 4 people
Preparation Time: 10 minutes
Ready Time: 20 minutes

Ingredients:
- 2 tablespoons extra-virgin olive oil
- 1 onion, chopped
- 2 cloves garlic, minced
- 2 cups cooked quinoa
- 1 cup cooked chickpeas
- 1 yellow bell pepper, diced
- 1 red bell pepper, diced
- 1 teaspoon garlic powder
- 1 teaspoon smoked paprika
- 2 cups kale, chopped
- 2 tablespoons lemon juice
- Kosher salt and freshly ground black pepper, to taste

Instructions:
1. Heat olive oil in a large skillet over medium heat.
2. Add onion and garlic; cook until translucent, about 3 minutes.
3. Add quinoa, chickpeas, bell peppers, garlic powder, paprika, and salt and pepper; cook until vegetables are softened, about 5 minutes.
4. Add kale and lemon juice; cook until kale is wilted, about 2 minutes.
5. Serve hot.

Nutrition information:
Calories: 295 kcal, Carbohydrates: 37 g, Protein: 11 g, Fat: 11 g, Saturated Fat: 2 g, Sodium: 116 mg, Potassium: 524 mg, Fiber: 7 g, Sugar: 3 g, Vitamin A: 2884 IU, Vitamin C: 83 mg, Calcium: 81 mg, Iron: 3 mg

89. Lemon Herb Baked Chicken Drumsticks

Lemon Herb Baked Chicken Drumsticks is an easy and delicious meal with the perfect balance of flavors and a hint of lemon. It is perfect for a weeknight dinner and perfect for entertaining.
Serving: 4
Preparation time: 10 minutes
Ready time: 45 minutes

Ingredients:
- 8 chicken drumsticks
- 1/4 cup lemon juice
- 2 cloves garlic, minced
- 2 teaspoons fresh rosemary, chopped
- 2 teaspoons fresh thyme leaves, chopped
- 2 teaspoons olive oil
- Salt and freshly ground pepper, to taste

Instructions:
1. Preheat the oven to 375°F.
2. In a medium bowl, combine the lemon juice, garlic, rosemary, thyme and olive oil.
3. Brush the chicken drumsticks with the lemon mixture and season with salt and pepper.

4. Place the drumsticks on a baking sheet and bake for 35 to 45 minutes or until cooked through and the juices run clear.

5. Remove from the oven and allow to cool before serving.

Nutrition information: per serving: 288 calories; 11g fat; 24g protein; 6g carbohydrates; 0g fiber; 2g sugar.

90. Ginger Turmeric Cauliflower Rice

Ginger Turmeric Cauliflower Rice is a delicious vegetarian side dish made from cooked cauliflower that is mixed with fresh-grated ginger and turmeric to create a flavorful, low-carbohydrate version of a classic rice dish.

Serving Size: 4
Preparation Time: 10 minutes
Ready Time: 25 minutes

Ingredients:
- 1 head cauliflower, grated or finely chopped
- 2 tablespoons olive oil
- 2 cloves garlic, minced
- 1 teaspoon grated fresh ginger
- 1 teaspoon ground turmeric
- Salt and pepper to taste

Instructions:
1. In a large skillet, heat the olive oil over medium-high heat.
2. Add the garlic, and sauté for 1 minute.
3. Add the cauliflower and sauté for 5 minutes.
4. Add the ginger and turmeric, and sauté for an additional 4 minutes.
5. Season with salt and pepper.
6. Serve hot.

Nutrition information:
Calories: 78 kcal, Carbohydrates: 8 g, Protein: 3 g, Fat: 5 g, Sodium: 37 mg, Potassium: 333 mg, Fiber: 3 g, Sugar: 3 g, Vitamin A: 15 IU, Vitamin C: 59.3 mg, Calcium: 28 mg, Iron: 0.7 mg

91. Roasted Brussels Sprouts and Quinoa Bowl

Enjoy the delicious combination of roasted Brussels sprouts and quinoa with this simple and healthy bowl. It's loaded with plenty of flavor and color and comes together quickly with minimal effort.

Serving: 4 servings
Preparation Time: 10 minutes
Ready in Time: 45 minutes

Ingredients:
- 2 cups Brussels sprouts, halved
- 2 tablespoons olive oil
- 1/2 teaspoon kosher salt
- Freshly ground black pepper, to taste
- 1 cup quinoa, cooked
- 1/2 cup feta cheese
- 2 tablespoons lemon juice
- 1 tablespoon chopped fresh mint (optional)

Instructions:
1. Preheat oven to 425°F. Line a baking sheet with parchment paper.
2. Place Brussels sprouts and olive oil on the baking sheet. Season with salt and pepper. Toss to combine.
3. Bake in the preheated oven for 25 minutes, stirring occasionally, or until the Brussels sprouts are golden brown and tender.
4. Transfer the roasted Brussels sprouts to a large bowl. Add the quinoa, feta, lemon juice, and mint. Gently toss to combine.
5. Serve roasted Brussels sprouts and quinoa hot or at room temperature.

Nutrition information:
- Calories: 218 kcal
- Carbohydrates: 20 g
- Protein: 6 g
- Fat: 12 g
- Saturated Fat: 3 g
- Cholesterol: 8 mg
- Sodium: 252 mg
- Potassium: 317 mg

- Fiber: 3 g
- Sugar: 2 g
- Vitamin A: 535 IU
- Vitamin C: 54.7 mg
- Calcium: 81 mg
- Iron: 2.5 mg

92. Mango Turmeric Chia Pudding

This delicious Mango Turmeric Chia Pudding is bursting with flavor and nutrition. It is a perfect on-the-go breakfast that can be prepared with minimal effort.
Serving: 4 servings
Preparation Time: 10 minutes
Ready Time: 4 hours

Ingredients:
- 2 large ripe mangoes
- ¼ cup white chia seeds
- 1 tablespoon ground turmeric
- 2 cups unsweetened almond milk
- 2 tablespoons maple syrup
- Optional: ½ teaspoon cardamom and/or ground ginger

Instructions:
1. Start by peeling the mangoes and adding them to a blender.
2. Puree the mangoes until smooth.
3. Transfer the mango puree to a medium bowl and add the chia seeds, turmeric, almond milk, maple syrup, and optional cardamom and/or ground ginger.
4. Stir all the Ingredients until combined.
5. Cover and refrigerate the pudding for at least 4 hours or overnight.

Nutrition information:
Serving size: ½ cup. The Mango Turmeric Chia Pudding contains around 160 calories, 7g fat, 20g carbs, 4g fiber, 11g sugar, and 4g protein.

93. Turmeric Grilled Shrimp Skewers

This recipe for Turmeric Grilled Shrimp Skewers is a delicious seafood dish perfect for a BBQ. Grilled to perfection, these shrimp skewers are full of flavor and come together easily for a wholesome summer meal.
Serving:
4 servings
Preparation time: 10 minutes
Ready time: 25 minutes

Ingredients:
- 16 large shrimp, peeled and deveined
- 5 tablespoons olive oil
- 2 teaspoons ground turmeric
- 1 teaspoon garlic powder
- 1 teaspoon smoked paprika
- ½ teaspoon cumin
- ½ teaspoon salt
- Juice of 1 lemon

Instructions:
1. Preheat an outdoor grill to high heat.
2. In a large bowl, combine the olive oil, turmeric, garlic powder, smoked paprika, cumin, salt and lemon juice.
3. Add the shrimp to the bowl and toss to coat.
4. Skewer the shrimp onto four metal or wooden skewers.
5. Place the skewers on the grill and cook 4-5 minutes per side, until cooked through.
6. Serve the skewers with lemon wedges.

Nutrition information:
Per Serving: 170 Calories; 11g Fat; 1g Carbohydrates; 16g Protein; 0.7g Fiber; 79mg Cholesterol.

94. Cucumber Avocado Spinach Salad

This refreshing and nutritious Cucumber Avocado Spinach Salad is an easy-to-make salad that is flavorful and filled with healthy Ingredients.

Serving: Serves 4 to 6
Preparation Time: 10 mins
Ready Time: 10 mins

Ingredients:
- 1 cucumber, peeled, seeds removed and diced
- 1 avocado, diced
- 2 cups baby spinach leaves
- 1/4 cup feta cheese
- 2 tablespoons extra-virgin olive oil
- 2 tablespoons freshly squeezed lemon juice
- 2 tablespoons fresh parsley, finely minced
- Sea salt, to taste
- Freshly ground black pepper, to taste

Instructions:
1. In a large bowl, combine cucumber, avocado, spinach, feta cheese, and parsley.
2. In a small bowl, whisk together olive oil and lemon juice. Pour over salad and toss to combine.
3. Season with salt and black pepper, to taste.
4. Serve immediately.

Nutrition information: Per serving: Calories 189; Total Fat 13.5g; Saturated fat 3.4g; Protein 4.7g; Total Carbohydrate 13.7g; Dietary Fiber 4.9g; Sugars 1.6g; Sodium 92mg

95. Lemon Garlic Herb Baked Turkey Breast

Introducing this mouthwatering Lemon Garlic Herb Baked Turkey Breast recipe! You won't regret cooking this tasty and flavourful turkey dish - it's perfect for a weeknight dinner or a potluck gathering with friends and family.
Serving: 6
Preparation time: 15 minutes
Ready time: 1 hour

Ingredients:

- 6-8 lbs turkey breast
- 3 cloves garlic, minced
- 1 lemon, juiced
- ¼ cup butter, melted
- 2 tablespoons olive oil
- 2 tablespoons herbs of your choice (Rosemary and Thyme work great)
- Salt and freshly ground pepper, to taste

Instructions:
1. Preheat oven to 375 F.
2. Place the turkey breast in a lightly greased roasting pan.
3. In a small bowl, mix together garlic, butter, olive oil, herbs, lemon juice, salt and pepper.
4. Rub the butter mixture all over the turkey.
5. Bake in oven for 45 minutes to an hour, or until a thermometer inserted into the thickest part of the turkey reads 165 F.
6. Allow the turkey to rest for 10 minutes before slicing.

Nutrition information:
Calories: 353; Fat: 15g; Cholesterol: 144mg; Sodium: 167mg; Carbohydrates: 1g; Protein: 52g

96. Ginger Turmeric Vegetable Curry

Ginger Turmeric Vegetable Curry is a flavourful, aromatic dish made with a mix of spices, vegetables and ginger and turmeric. It's a vegan and gluten-free meal that is perfect for weeknight dinners and is sure to please everyone's taste buds.
Serving: 4
Preparation time: 10 minutes
Ready time: 40 minutes

Ingredients:
- 2 tablespoons of olive oil
- 1 onion, diced
- 2 cloves garlic, minced
- 2 teaspoons of freshly grated ginger
- 2 teaspoons of ground turmeric

- 1 teaspoon of ground cumin
- 1 teaspoon of ground coriander
- ½ teaspoon of cayenne
- 1 can (14.5 oz/400 g) of diced tomatoes
- 1 can (14.5 oz/400 g) of chickpeas, drained and rinsed
- 1 zucchini, sliced
- 2 cups of spinach
- 1 cup of cooked brown rice

Instructions:

1. Heat the olive oil in a large saucepan over medium-high heat.
2. Add the onion and cook until softened, about 5 minutes.
3. Add the garlic, ginger, turmeric, cumin, coriander, and cayenne and cook until fragrant, about 1 minute.
4. Add the diced tomatoes, chickpeas, zucchini and stir.
5. Reduce the heat to low and simmer for 20 minutes.
6. Add the spinach and cook for 5 minutes more.
7. Serve over cooked brown rice.

Nutrition information:

Calories: 344.6 | Protein: 7.3 g | Total Fat: 6.6 g | Sodium: 78.4 mg | Total Carbohydrate: 57.4 g | Dietary Fiber: 10.9 g | Sugars: 6.1 g | Calcium: 77.3 mg | Iron: 5.3 mg

CONCLUSION

Simply Anti-Inflammatory: 96 Easy 5-Ingredient Recipes is a great cookbook that provides simple and delicious recipes that are designed to reduce inflammation in the body. These recipes use only 5 ingredients or fewer, meaning they are easy to prepare. The book includes recipes that are suitable for vegetarians or vegans, and also has meal suggestions for special diets such as ketogenic and low-carbohydrate diets. Moreover, each recipe is accompanied by nutritional information that provides an understanding of how the combination of ingredients can be beneficial for fighting inflammation and promoting general health.

Overall, Simply Anti-Inflammatory: 96 Easy 5-Ingredient Recipes is an outstanding cookbook with great recipes that are simple to prepare, but packed with nutrition. It is a wonderful resource for anyone wanting to incorporate more anti-inflammatory foods into their lifestyle and maintain their overall health. All of the recipes in the book are delicious and healthful, and come together to create a tasty meal that is both nourishing and fulfilling. Whether you are a beginner, intermediate, or advanced cook, this cookbook is sure to provide you with plenty of mouth-watering dishes to keep your taste buds satisfied. So, if you're looking for a cookbook with delicious and nutritious recipes to help reduce inflammation and keep you healthy, this is the book for you.

Printed in Great Britain
by Amazon